Framework

RE

Steve Clarke

2

Hodder Murray

1·2007

The Publishers would like to thank the following for permission to reproduce copyright material:

Photo credits p.9 Bury Peerless; **p.12** (used twice) Rex Features/Robin Hume; **p.15** 1 Corbis/Neal Preston, 2 Corbis/Annie Griffiths Belt, 3 Corbis/Zen Icknow, 4 Rex Features/Frances Dean, 5 Rex Features/Israel Images, 6 World Religions Photo Library/Christine Osborne; **p.16** t Corbis/W. Perry Conway, m Corbis/Craig Tuttle, b Photodisc; **p.18** World Religions Photo Library/Christine Osborne; **p.19** b Corbis/Alinari Archives, t World Religions Photo Library/Christine Osborne; **p.22** l Corbis/Swim Ink 2 LLC, 1 Corbis/Jon Feingersh, 2 Corbis/Leland Bobbé, 3 Empics/Matthew Fearn/PA, 4 Photolibrary.com/Workbook Inc; **p.28** l Science Photo Library/Kenneth Libbrecht, r Photodisc; **p.29** Corbis/Stefano Bianchetti; **p.31** Art Archive/British Museum/Eileen Tweedy; **p.32** l Rex Features/Frederic Aranda, m Corbis/Ted Spiegel, r Empics/Belinda Rolland; **p.37** t World Religions Photo Library/Christine Osborne, bl World Religions Photo Library/Christine Osborne, br Rex Features/Image Source; **p.38** t & r World Religions Photo Library/Christine Osborne, l Bridgeman Art Library/Victoria & Albert Museum London UK; **p.39** courtesy and kind permission of Amnesty International, UNICEF and BLISS; **p.42** Rex Features; **p.44** l Empics/PA, r Rex Features/Action Press; **p.48** tl Action Plus Photographic/Glyn Kirk, tm Corbis/Catherine Panchout, tr Science Photo Library/Michael Donne, bl Rex Features/Alexander Caminada, bm Getty Images/Xavier Bonghi, br Empics/PA; **p.52** tl Getty Images/AFP, bl Alamy/Sally & Richard Greenhill, tr Corbis/Zainal Abd Halim/Reuters, br Circa Photo Library/ICOREC; **p.53** l Rex Features/Israel Images, r World Religions Photo Library /Christine Osborne; **p.54** t Art Archive/British Library, b Photodisc; **p.55** tr Corbis/Peter Johnson, tl Corbis/Craig Lovell, br Corbis/Ashley Cooper, bl World Religions Photo Library/Christine Osborne; **p.63** 2 Corbis/Roger Ressmeyer, 3 Alamy/Israel Images, 4 Rex Features/Israel Images, 5 TopFoto/Larry Kolvoord/The Image Works, 6 TopFoto/James Nubile/The Image Works; **p.64** tl Rex Features/ F. Sierakowski, A Corbis/Dave Bartruff, B Bridgeman Art Library/Jewish Museum London, C Corbis/Elio Ciol, D Photodisc; **p.71** Corbis/Archivo Iconografico, S.A.; **p.72** Corbis/Angelo Hornak; **p.73** Corbis/David Cumming/Eye Ubiquitous; **p.77** World Religions Photo Library/Christine Osborne; **p.79** World Religions Photo Library/Christine Osborne; **p.82** l, r & mr Photodisc, ml Hodder; **p.83** Art Archive/Museo del Prado Madrid/ Joseph Martin; **p.90** Science Photo Library/Tek Image; **p.92** Empics/Gesang Dawa/AP; **p.93** World Religions Photo Library/Claire Stout; **p.95** Corbis/ Alinari Archives; **p.99** 1 Corbis/Janez Skok, 2 World Religions Photo Library/Christine Osborne, 3 Corbis/Historical Picture Archive; **p.102** 1 Rex Features/Keystone USA, 2 Corbis/Chris Lisle, 3 Corbis/Morton Beebe, 4 Corbis/Bruce Burkhardt, 5 Rex Features/Sabah Arar; **p.103** 6 World Religions Photo Library/Christine Osborne, 7 Rex Features/Francis Dean, 8 Corbis/Tim Page, A Rex Features, B Action Plus Photographic, C Rex Features/David Hartley, D Empics/Jan Bauer/AP, E Getty Images/Stephane De Sakutin, F Corbis/Michael S. Yamashita, G Getty Images/Tim Graham, H Corbis/Sian Touhig; **p.105** World Religions Photo Library/Christine Osborne; **p.107** t Corbis/Chris Lisle, b Corbis/Brian A. Vikander; **p.111** t Corbis/Joel Stettenheim, b Getty Images/Cris Bouroncle; **p.115** World Religions Photo Library/Christine Osborne; **p.116** l Corbis/Leif Skoogfors, r Rex Features/ Sipa Press; **p.117** t, m & b Getty Images/Time & Life Pictures; **p.118** Dalai Lama Corbis/Jim Bourg/Reuters, Ambedkar Corbis/Bettmann, King Rex Features/Everett Collection, Romero Corbis/Leif Skoogfors, Bhaktivedanta Corbis/Bettmann, Gandhi Illustrated London News, Malcolm X TopFoto/AP; **p.119** Yusuf Islam Rex Features/Richard Young, Hertzl Corbis/Bettmann, Wiesenthal Rex Features/Karl Schoendorfer, Bhindranwale Corbis/Bettmann, Singh Corbis/Brooks Kraft, Marley Rex Features, Fry TopFoto/The British Library/HIP.

Acknowledgements Amana Books for extracts from the *Surah (Qur'an)* (adapted from *The Meaning of the Holy Qur'an* ed. Abdullah Yusuf Ali, 1998); Bertrams Print On Demand for extracts from *The Upanishads* (translated by F. Max Muller, *Sacred Books of the East* (Vol. 1) 1879); the Buddha Dharma Education Association, Inc for extracts from the *Dancing Peacock Story* (adapted from *Buddhist Tales for Young and Old* (Vol. 1) by Todd Anderson, 1992) and the *Dhammapada* (adapted from the *Dhammapada, Buddha's Path of Wisdom* tr. Ven. Acharya Buddharakkita, 1992), www.buddhanet.net; the Sikhism Home Page for extracts from *Guru Nanak and Guru Granth Sahib*.

The publishers would also like to thank the following:
Columbia University Press for the extract from *Islam in America*, Jane Smith, 1999; the Dharma Realm Buddhist Association for the Tipitaka quote from *Sutra in Forty-Two Sections*, 1977; HarperCollins for the Richard Dawkins quotes from *River Out of Eden: A Darwinian View of Life*, 1995; Hodder (scripture quotations taken from the HOLY BIBLE, NEW INTERNATIONAL VERSION. Copyright © 1973, 1978, 1984 by International Bible Society. Used by permission of Hodder & Stoughton Publishers, A member of the Hodder Headline Group. All rights reserved. "NIV" is a registered trademark of International Bible Society. UK trademark number 1448790.); SGI-USA for the Tipitaka quote from the *Writings of Nichiren Daishonin*, 2004; Viva (Vegetarians International Voice for Animals) for the extract from www.viva.org.uk; the Wall Street Journal for the Charles Townes quotes, March 11 2005.

Every effort has been made to trace all copyright holders, but if any have been inadvertently overlooked the Publishers will be pleased to make the necessary arrangements at the first opportunity.

Although every effort has been made to ensure that website addresses are correct at time of going to press, Hodder Murray cannot be held responsible for the content of any website mentioned in this book. It is sometimes possible to find a relocated web page by typing in the address of the home page for a website in the URL window of your browser.

Papers used in this book are natural, renewable and recyclable products. They are made from wood grown in sustainable forests. The logging and manufacturing processes conform to the environmental regulations of the country of origin.

Orders: please contact Bookpoint Ltd, 130 Milton Park, Abingdon, Oxon OX14 4SB. Telephone: (44) 01235 827720. Fax: (44) 01235 400454. Lines are open from 9.00–6.00, Monday to Saturday, with a 24-hour message answering service. Visit our website at www.hoddereducation.co.uk.

CR
200
CLA

Contents

UNIT 1: CAN RELIGION BE TRUE?

Lesson 1: What is the difference between knowing and believing?

◎ Learn what it means to know something, and what it means to believe something.

◎ Find out about the three conditions of knowledge.

◎ Discover why religious people claim to know about God.

Lesson 2: What is belief?

◎ Read about the three characteristics of belief.

◎ Work out a definition of the word 'belief'.

◎ Apply some beliefs to real-life situations.

Lesson 3: What is truth?

◎ Work out a definition of the word 'truth'.

◎ Test whether certain statements are true or false.

◎ Find out about four types of truth.

Lesson 4: What counts as evidence?

◎ Learn about the different types of evidence that support different types of truth.

◎ Decide what makes good evidence.

◎ Discover the problems with evidence.

◎ Find out why some truths do not require formal evidence.

Lesson 5: What makes an experience religious?

◎ Think about how people experience feelings.

◎ Find out about words that can be used to describe religious experiences.

◎ Discover how religious people encourage religious experiences.

◎ Identify how religious people explain their experiences.

Lesson 6: So, is religion true?

◎ Find out some different ideas about truth.

◎ Discuss whether truth may be absolute, relative or subjective.

◎ Review the three different religious attitudes learned last year: exclusivist, inclusivist and pluralist.

◎ Consider how the meaning of the word 'true' affects beliefs about whether religion is true.

1. What is the difference between knowing and believing?

SKILLS

- **thinking about** what we mean by knowing and believing
- **distinguishing between** statements of knowledge and belief
- **presenting** an argument on a certain subject
- **working out** your thoughts on knowledge and belief

Belief is a very important part of religion. In this lesson we shall start to look at what belief is by examining the differences between believing something and knowing it.

ACTIVITY ONE ....

1. Write two lists. The first list should consist of five things that you know; the second list should be five things that you believe.

2. Discuss your lists with a partner. Try to decide between you what the difference is between knowing and believing.

KEY WORDS

Argument   the statement of a belief backed up by reasons

Evidence   a collection of reasons

Reason   a statement used to back up an opinion, belief or statement of knowledge

ⓘ What does it mean to know something?

In your discussion, you may have reached the following conclusions:

1. If you know something, you must believe it. It would be daft to say:

> I know that London is the capital of England, but I don't believe it.

On the other hand, if you believe something, you don't have to know it.

2. If you know something, it must be true. For example, you can't claim to know that England won the football World Cup in 2002, because they didn't. However, if you believe something, it may or may not be true.

3. If you know something, you must have **evidence**. You must be able to back up whatever you claim to know with good **reasons**.

ACTIVITY TWO ....

Do these people know or believe? Fill in the missing words. Discuss your answers with a partner. Remember to be prepared to give reasons for your opinions.

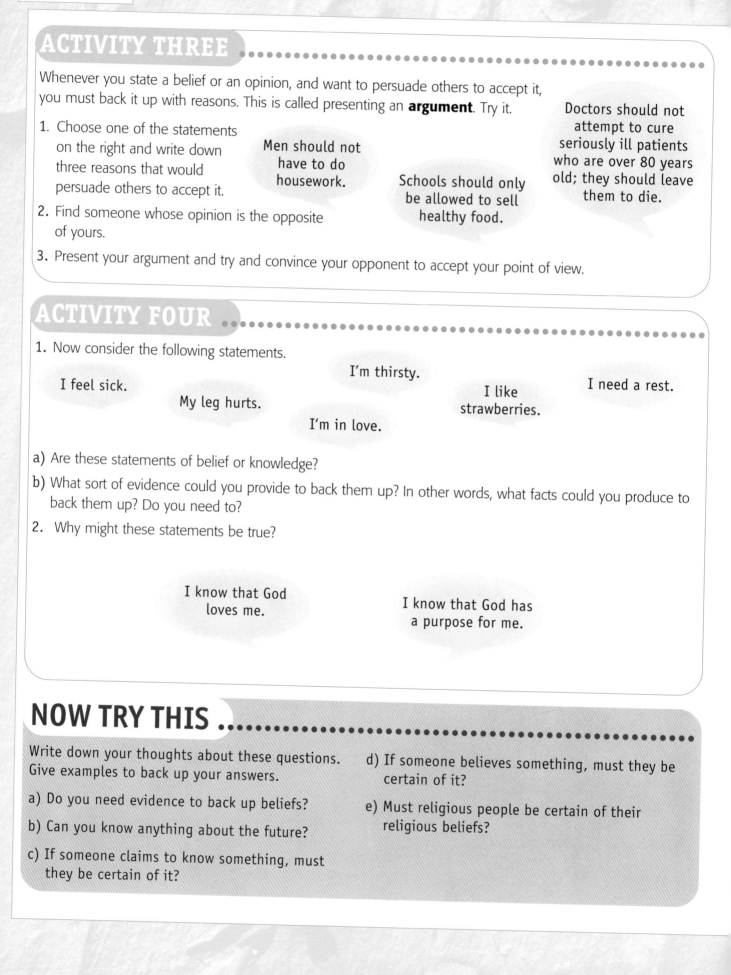

ACTIVITY THREE

Whenever you state a belief or an opinion, and want to persuade others to accept it, you must back it up with reasons. This is called presenting an **argument**. Try it.

1. Choose one of the statements on the right and write down three reasons that would persuade others to accept it.

2. Find someone whose opinion is the opposite of yours.

3. Present your argument and try and convince your opponent to accept your point of view.

Men should not have to do housework.

Schools should only be allowed to sell healthy food.

Doctors should not attempt to cure seriously ill patients who are over 80 years old; they should leave them to die.

ACTIVITY FOUR

1. Now consider the following statements.

I feel sick.

My leg hurts.

I'm in love.

I'm thirsty.

I like strawberries.

I need a rest.

a) Are these statements of belief or knowledge?

b) What sort of evidence could you provide to back them up? In other words, what facts could you produce to back them up? Do you need to?

2. Why might these statements be true?

I know that God loves me.

I know that God has a purpose for me.

NOW TRY THIS ...

Write down your thoughts about these questions. Give examples to back up your answers.

a) Do you need evidence to back up beliefs?

b) Can you know anything about the future?

c) If someone claims to know something, must they be certain of it?

d) If someone believes something, must they be certain of it?

e) Must religious people be certain of their religious beliefs?

2. What is belief?

SKILLS

- **comparing** knowledge and belief
- **providing reasons** to support opinions
- **inferring** what actions might result from some beliefs
- **linking** beliefs with actions

ACTIVITY ONE ·······················

Using what you learned about the differences between knowing and believing in the last lesson, try to write a definition of the word 'belief' that compares believing with knowing.

You don't have to be religious to have beliefs. Everyone has them.

I believe that violence never solves anything.

I believe poor diet and lack of exercise are making the people of Britain unhealthy.

I believe that liars always get found out.

ACTIVITY TWO ······················

If you believe that students should not have to wear school uniform, your reasons might be (i) that it is too expensive for some parents to buy, and (ii) that it does not allow you to express your individuality.

Look at the person below stating her beliefs.

a) What sort of reasons could she offer to back up her beliefs? Give two examples for each.

b) What would make each belief true?

ⓘ What makes something a belief?

These are the characteristics that a belief has:

1. A belief is a private state of mind. It involves thinking about an idea, and agreeing or disagreeing with it.

2. You don't have to have evidence to believe something. A belief for which you can provide no reasons is called an **irrational** belief. On the other hand, the more evidence you have to support a belief, the more likely it is to be true.

3. If you believe in something, you have to be prepared to act as if it were true. For example, if you believe it is wrong for human beings to kill animals, you would be a vegetarian and you wouldn't wear leather or fur.

Did you include these in your definition in Activity One?

KEY WORD

Irrational   having no reasons

ACTIVITY THREE

1. Choose one of the following statements of belief:

Smoking cigarettes should be against the law.

No family should have more than one car.

People in Britain should be allowed to carry guns.

Now say:

a) whether you agree or disagree with the statement,

b) what reasons you have to back up your opinion.

2. How could someone act on the statements above? Give two examples for each.

3. How would you argue *against* each of these statements? Remember that you must provide reasons in order to present an argument.

If you see a list of rules or laws about how to act, you can be sure that they reflect a set of beliefs. For example, your school may have a list of rules for students to follow. These rules do not appear from nowhere. They are based on beliefs. They are examples of how a set of beliefs can be put into practice. These beliefs may be written down in a school charter.

School Charter

We believe that every member of this school has the right:

A To be treated with respect.

B To have their possessions respected.

C To work in safe and pleasant surroundings.

D To be enabled to succeed.

We believe that every member of this school has the duty to secure these rights for every other member.

SCHOOL RULES

Ground rules for behaviour:

1. Put litter in litter bins.
2. Bring appropriate equipment to each lesson.
3. Move around the school in a quiet and orderly fashion.
4. Ask before you borrow another person's property.
5. Speak courteously to others.
6. Listen to others when they are speaking.
7. Ask if you need help.
8. Take lost property to the school office.

ACTIVITY FOUR

Look at the beliefs set out in the school charter and the list of school rules. Which rules come from which beliefs? Match them up.

All of this, of course, applies to religious beliefs as well.

I believe in karma:
if you do good to others,
then good things will
happen to you.

I believe that
I will be reborn
in another body
after my death.

I believe that
God forgives everyone
who is truly sorry for
what they have done
wrong.

I believe that the
land we call Israel
was promised to us
by God.

I believe that God has
spoken to us through his
holy book, the Qur'an.

NOW TRY THIS ....

How could the people in the pictures above put
their beliefs into practice? For example, if you
believed that good things would happen to you if
you did good things for others, how would it
affect the way you lived your life? Discuss your
ideas with a partner.

I believe that
everyone has equal
value, regardless of
religion, race or sex.

3. What is truth?

ACTIVITY ONE

Decide which of the following statements are true.

a) Henry VIII had six wives.

b) Snow is white.

c) Adolf Hitler was German.

d) Stockholm is the capital of Norway.

e) There is life after death.

f) Fish breathe in carbon dioxide.

g) It is wrong to steal.

h) Smoking kills.

i) There is a purpose to life.

j) Adolf Hitler was an evil man.

k) People can change.

ACTIVITY TWO

Go through your answers to the statements in Activity One with a partner. Discuss what people generally mean when they say that something is true. Can you agree on a definition? Here are some possible definitions to help you in your discussion.

- A statement is true if it corresponds with the facts.
- A statement is true if everyone agrees with it.
- A statement is true if it works.
- A statement is true if you think it is.

ⓘ Types of truth

When we are dealing with truth, it is easier to say that there are different types of truth.

1. The first category consists of statements that describe the world around us. Such statements are called **empirical**. Scientific truths are examples of empirical truths.

2. Statements about the past are known as historical truths.

3. **Moral** statements are statements about what is good or bad, or right or wrong. They are about how human beings ought and ought not to behave.

4. **Spiritual** statements are concerned with the parts of human life that people experience, but not with their physical senses. They include statements about emotions and feelings, such as love or freedom.

ACTIVITY THREE

On the following page is a selection of statements that some people claim to be true. But what types of truth are they? For each one, say whether it is empirical, historical, moral or spiritual.

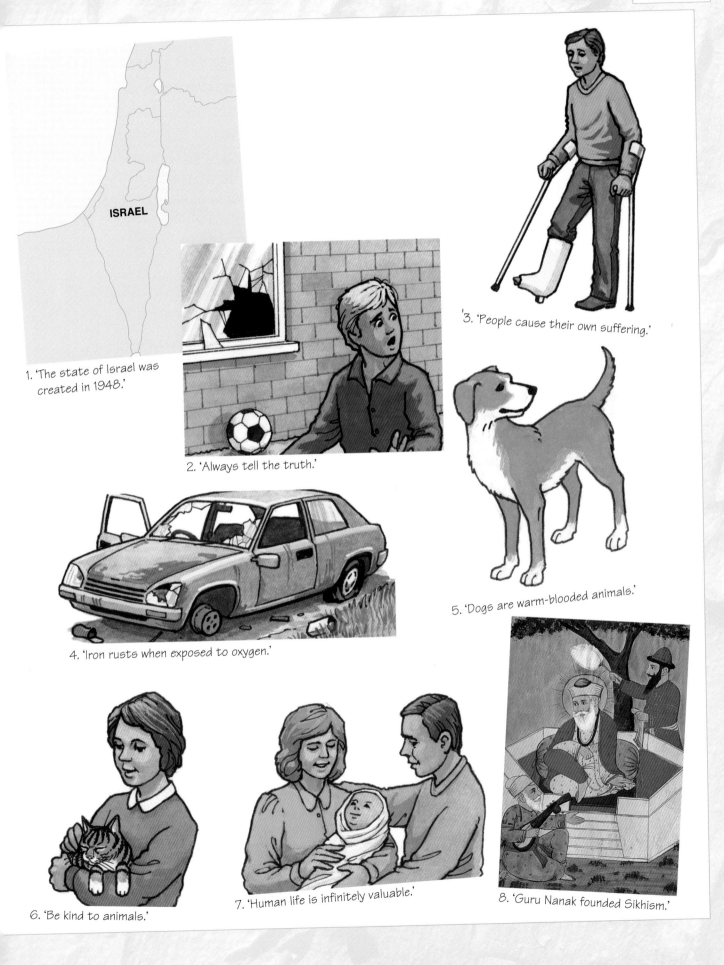

1. 'The state of Israel was created in 1948.'

2. 'Always tell the truth.'

3. 'People cause their own suffering.'

4. 'Iron rusts when exposed to oxygen.'

5. 'Dogs are warm-blooded animals.'

6. 'Be kind to animals.'

7. 'Human life is infinitely valuable.'

8. 'Guru Nanak founded Sikhism.'

ACTIVITY FOUR ....

1. Can you show that the following statements are true? How would you do it? What sorts of reasons and evidence do you need to support these statements?

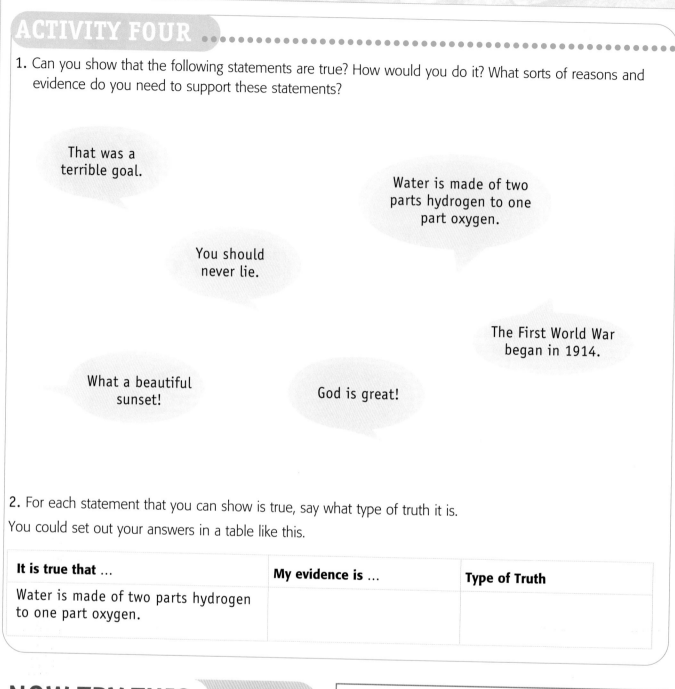

That was a terrible goal.

Water is made of two parts hydrogen to one part oxygen.

You should never lie.

The First World War began in 1914.

What a beautiful sunset!

God is great!

2. For each statement that you can show is true, say what type of truth it is.

You could set out your answers in a table like this.

It is true that ...	My evidence is ...	Type of Truth
Water is made of two parts hydrogen to one part oxygen.		

NOW TRY THIS ....

Think of your own examples of the four types of truth. Ask a partner how they would test each one to see if it is true.

KEY WORDS

Empirical provable through observation and experiment

Moral to do with what is good, bad, right or wrong in human behaviour

Spiritual to do with aspects of human life that cannot be experienced physically, like emotions and feelings

4. What counts as evidence?

SKILLS

- **ranking** evidence
- **evaluating** evidence
- **separating** opinions from facts
- **empathising** with the feelings of others

In your lessons so far, you have learned that:

- If you claim to know something, it must be true.
- If you claim to know something, you must be able to provide evidence.
- There are different types of truth.

Each of the four types of truth requires a different type of evidence.

ⓘ Empirical truth

Empirical truths are tested by conducting experiments. For example, scientists make a **hypothesis** (a prediction about what the result of their experiments will be), and then conduct the experiments to provide evidence to prove or disprove the hypothesis.

ACTIVITY ONE ·················

What evidence do you have that water expands when it is frozen? On the right there are four pieces of evidence. Which is the best?

1. Put the four pieces of evidence in rank order, and explain the reasons for your decisions.
2. Does the evidence prove the hypothesis?
3. How could each of the pieces of evidence be wrong?

Hypothesis: Water expands when it is frozen

<u>Evidence:</u>

1

I can see it does.

2

Scientists say it does.

3

My mum says it does.

4

I can see the effects of it.

ⓘ Historical truth

Statements about the past can be tested by referring to historical records or artefacts. The trouble is, though, that it is often impossible to judge how reliable these records are.

ACTIVITY TWO ················

Here is part of an account of the Battle of Hastings, when Duke William of Normandy defeated England's King Harold.

William led his troops with great skill, halting them when they turned to retreat, giving them courage and sharing in their danger. He always led them, rather than ordering them to go on ahead. It is absolutely clear that it was the Duke's bravery that inspired his soldiers to advance and gave them courage.

1. Which of the words and phrases in this account are facts, and which are the writer's own opinions?

2. Look at the two headlines from different newspapers. What words do they use to present the same event in different ways? Can you know which is the 'true account'? How reliable do you think newspaper articles are as a piece of evidence?

Can you ever be sure what happened?

VICTORY FOR UNITED AS SMITH SMASHES CITY'S DEFENCE

UNITED SCRAPE THROUGH AS SMITH SCORES LUCKY GOAL

ⓘ Moral truth

Moral truths are about how we, as human beings, ought and ought not to behave. People have different ideas about what evidence is needed for moral truths. Some say that something is right if it makes the greatest number of people happy. Some say that God has revealed to human beings what is right. Still others say that what is right is different for different people in different situations.

ACTIVITY THREE ....

1. It is wrong to murder. It is also against the law.

   Can you think of other examples of laws in Britain that are based on moral rules?

2. It is wrong to have an affair if you are married; but it is not against the law.

   Can you think of more examples of moral statements that many British people agree about that are not laws?

3. Imagine a society without laws. What would it be like?

ⓘ Spiritual truth

Spiritual truths are, perhaps, the trickiest of all. Religious people sometimes talk about faith. They mean they have complete trust in the spiritual truths they hold. If you have faith in a person and trust them completely, you do so based on your past experiences of them. You do not need evidence for your trust. It is built on your feelings about the person. In the same way, some religious people would say that they do not need evidence for spiritual truths. They are truths that are felt inside, and cannot be measured from the outside.

ACTIVITY FOUR ....

Describe how people may feel in the following situations:

a) looking at the sun setting

b) hearing someone say, 'I love you'

c) seeing their first grandchild

d) winning a national music competition

e) being let out of prison

f) seeing a friend get hurt.

So what is truth?

It seems, then, that nothing can be proved to be true. You can have evidence for something, and the more evidence you have, the more likely it is to be true. But different kinds of truth require different kinds of evidence. It is not always appropriate to use scientific methods to find the truth of spiritual statements.

NOW TRY THIS ....

a) Try to write a definition of the word 'spiritual'.

b) What evidence is there for the existence of the human spirit?

c) Do you have to be religious to believe in the spirit? Give reasons for your answer.

KEY WORDS

Artefact   a human-made object

Hypothesis   a scientific theory or prediction

5. What makes an experience religious?

SKILLS

- **expressing** your emotions and feelings
- **analysing** accounts of religious experiences
- **linking** feelings to religious activities
- **explaining** what spiritual experiences mean to religious people

ACTIVITY ONE ••••••••••••••••

Listen to the pieces of music your teacher plays to you. Write down words that each piece suggests to you. They could be feelings, colours, scenes or situations.

We all have spiritual experiences. They can come from listening to a piece of music, seeing something beautiful, being with a loved one, or even experiencing suffering. For religious people, spiritual experiences convince them of the truth of their beliefs.

ⓘ Religious experiences

Here are some examples of experiences that changed people's lives.

Buddhism

As a result of seeing old age, sickness and death in people, Siddhartha Gautama realised that suffering is an unavoidable part of life. When he saw a holy man, he became determined to find an answer to the problem of suffering.

Christianity

In the Judean desert, Jesus struggled with a choice between a life of selfishness and one of service.

Islam

Muhammad heard the words of the Qur'an revealed to him in a desert cave. He was both frightened and **empowered**.

Judaism

Moses was **overawed** when he felt the presence of God in a burning bush. He was humbled and aware of something special. He was inspired to free the Israelite people from slavery.

Sikhism

Guru Nanak's life changed when he came to understand that all people are connected as God's creation.

ACTIVITY TWO ••••••••••••••••

1. Read the accounts of religious experiences in the boxes above. Write a list of all the verbs that are used.
2. Use the words in your list to help you write an account of what religious experiences are like.

All people, whether they are religious or not, have experiences when they learn great truths about life. Religious people take part in activities that encourage such experiences.

1

A Buddhist meditating

2

An adult Christian being baptised

3

A Hindu funeral

4

Muslims studying the Qu'ran

5

A Jewish family celebrating Pesach

6

Sikhs erecting a khanda flagpole

ACTIVITY THREE •••••••••••••••••••••••••••••••••••••

Look carefully at the pictures of religious activities above.

1. Describe what you see in each photograph.

2. Which of the following words would best fit each photograph?

togetherness   peace   sadness   joy   pride   wisdom

3. Explain why you chose these words, and how each activity in the photos could produce these experiences.

15

ACTIVITY FOUR

One of the things that makes a spiritual experience a religious one is the way in which it is explained.

1. How might a religious person explain these sights? What might they feel about them?

2. How might a non-religious person explain them? What might they feel?

NOW TRY THIS

In 1964, African-American boxer Cassius Clay became a Muslim and changed his name to Muhammad Ali. After he performed the hajj, the Muslim pilgrimage to Makkah in Saudi Arabia, he described his experience in this way.

'I have had many nice moments in my life. But the feeling I had while standing on Mount Arafat [just outside Makkah] on the day of the hajj, was the most unique. I felt lifted by the indescribable spiritual atmosphere there as over one and a half million pilgrims asked God to forgive them for their sins and give them His choicest blessings.

It was a thrilling experience to see people belonging to different colours, races and nationalities, kings, heads of state and ordinary men from very poor countries all clad in two simple white sheets praying to God without any sense of either pride or inferiority.

It was a practical demonstration of the concept of equality in Islam.'

(*Islam in America*, Jane Smith)

a) Explain what effect Muhammad Ali's experience might have had on his life.

b) How might a non-religious person explain Muhammad Ali's experience?

c) Is his experience true?

d) In your opinion, does Muhammad Ali's experience provide evidence for the existence of God?

KEY WORDS
Empowered   given power and authority
Overawed   filled with fear and wonder

16

6. So, is religion true?

SKILLS

- **giving examples** of different types of words
- **classifying** words according to type
- **matching** similar ideas
- **expressing** your own opinions about religions and truth
- **presenting an argument** to back up your opinions

ⓘ What is the meaning of some words?

An adjective is a describing word. The word 'true' is an adjective.

When we try to define adjectives, we find that there are different types.

- Some words have meanings that are **absolute**. This means that their meanings are fixed and cannot change. They include *square* and *blue*. It doesn't matter who uses the words, or when they say them: they always mean the same thing. There is only one real meaning.

- Some words have meanings that are **relative**. Their meanings change according to what you're talking about. Words like *big* or *soft* are relative. Is an elephant big or small? It all depends on what you're comparing it to. In a way, big and small are not separate words: they are at opposite ends of the same scale.

- Some words have meanings that are **subjective**. The meanings of these words depend on who is saying them. Words like *funny* or *beautiful* have subjective meanings. What is funny to me may not be funny to you.

KEY WORDS

Absolute   fixed or set
Relative   changeable when compared to different things
Subjective   individual

ACTIVITY ONE ....

1. Which group of adjective do the following words belong to?

    soft   British   old

    stupid   left-handed

    cruel   loud   daily

    normal   true

2. Add two more adjectives to each of the three types.

Did you find it difficult to work out which type of word 'true' belongs to? Don't worry: people can't agree about it. Some say its meaning is absolute, some that it is relative, and some that it is subjective.

ACTIVITY TWO ....

Last year you may have learned that some people are *exclusivist*: they believe that theirs is the only true religion; other people are *inclusivist*: they say that all religions share the truth – they are all on the same scale; and some other people are *pluralist*: they claim that all religions are true to those who believe them.

1. Pair up the words on the left with those on the right.

    relative   exclusivist

    absolute   inclusivist

    subjective   pluralist

2. How did you choose which word to match with which?

So, all religious people claim that religion is true, but they don't all agree what truth means!

ACTIVITY THREE

1. Which of the following statements would you agree with?

All religions are
expressing the
same truth.

No religion is
true.

Only one religion can
be right; the rest must
be wrong.

Each religion is true
to its followers.

2. Give at least two reasons to support your claim.

ACTIVITY FOUR

Below and on the opposite page are quotations from three leaders of three faiths.

Work out which statement reveals an attitude that is exclusivist, which inclusivist, and which pluralist.

▶ *'There is no difference between ... a Hindu and a Muslim. Though differences seem to mark and distinguish ... such differences are trivial.'* **Guru Gobind Singh** *(Sikhism)*

◀ *'Work out your own path to enlightenment.'* Siddhartha Gautama (Buddhism)

▶ *'I am the way, the truth and the life. No one reaches (God) the Father, except through me.'* **Jesus (John 14:6) (Christianity)**

NOW TRY THIS ...

Do people follow a religion because they believe it is true, or do they believe it is true because they are brought up to follow it? Here are some examples, what do they suggest?

- St Paul was a Jew but became a Christian when he saw a vision of Jesus.

- Sarah is Jewish because she was brought up to be.

- Michael had a religious upbringing, but is not now religious.

19

SUMMARY OF UNIT 1

Lesson 2

You have learned what makes something a belief, and how beliefs affect people's lives.

Lesson 3

You have learned what makes something true, and that there are four different types of truth.

Lesson 1

You have learned what the differences are between knowing something and believing it, and what the three conditions of knowledge are.

Can religion be true?

Lesson 4

You have learned that different types of truth require different types of evidence, and what the types of evidence are.

Lesson 6

You have learned why it is difficult to define what is true, and how this makes it difficult to say whether religion is true.

Lesson 5

You have learned what spiritual experiences are, and how religious people explain them.

UNIT 2: HOW IS RELIGION TRUE?

Lesson 1: How do people see the world?

◎ What is a world-view?

◎ Find out where our world-views come from.

◎ Describe your own world-view.

◎ Discover how different people have different world-views.

Lesson 2: How do beliefs affect people's world-views?

◎ What are ultimate questions?

◎ Find out how we interpret different world-views.

◎ Understand how beliefs contribute to world-views.

Lesson 3: What has science got to do with religion?

◎ Find out what religion and science have in common, and how they differ.

◎ Learn about the history of science and religion.

◎ Work out how to use scientific knowledge.

◎ Interpret quotations about science and religion.

Lesson 4: Can religion and science agree?

◎ Find out about different views on the relationship between science and religion.

◎ Analyse different points of view; religious, scientific and both.

◎ Discover different ways of interpreting the Bible.

Lesson 5: Can religion make sense of the world?

◎ Read and interpret an allegory.

◎ Discuss the purpose of life.

◎ Read about some religious views on the purpose of life and compare them.

Lesson 6: How does religion make sense of the world?

◎ Find out why religious people believe that human life is sacred.

◎ Discover how people put their beliefs about the sanctity of life into practice.

◎ Design a symbol to represent the belief in the sanctity of life.

1. How do people see the world?

SKILLS

- **discussing** how people learn aspects of their culture
- **classifying** the sources of aspects of culture
- **analysing** your own world-view
- **investigating** other people's world-views
- **comparing** world-views

▶ *You can see things in different ways. Do you see a young lady or an old woman in this picture?*

At Christmas time, many people in Britain put a turkey in the oven and sit by the fire with their pet dog. They think this is normal. But what would we think of someone who put a dog in the oven and sat by the fire with their pet turkey?

The view you have of something depends on where you are when you look at it. The country we inhabit, the culture we are born into, and the time we live in all influence the way we see the world and react to it. It is called our **world-view**. Each of us has a slightly different world-view, because each of us has different influences.

ACTIVITY ONE

Discuss these questions with a partner.

1. Why do men and boys tend to have short hair, while women and girls have long hair?

2. Why do Chinese people use chopsticks to eat with?

3. Why do British people queue at bus stops?

4. Why do some people put up a tree in their homes at Christmas time?

Is the fork on the left of the plate? It all depends on where you are when you look at it.

ⓘ What influences our world-view?

Our world-view is formed by the influence of:

- our families

- educational institutions (like schools and universities)

- the media (such as newspapers, magazines, television, radio and the internet)

- peers (people of our own age group)

- places of work

- religious institutions (for example churches, mosques and synagogues).

Many religious people claim that their knowledge of God and ethics (what is right and wrong) come to them from God. We shall consider this in greater detail in Unit Six.

ACTIVITY TWO

Where do we learn:

1. that water is made of two parts hydrogen and one part oxygen?

2. how to clean our teeth?

3. that killing is wrong?

4. how to cook lemon chicken?

5. how to speak?

6. that men should not cry?

7. what is fashionable?

8. that we should queue at bus stops?

9. that Henry VIII had six wives?

10. that the boss is always right (even if they are wrong!)?

11. that we should hold doors open for others?

12. that boys don't wear dresses?

13. which trainers are not cool?

14. that we should treat others as we would like to be treated?

15. that we should drink only clean water?

16. how to use a knife and fork?

17. the story of Christmas?

18. what music to listen to?

19. about what may happen after death?

20. how to climb a ladder safely?

ⓘ World-views and religions

Religions themselves are world-views, though, of course, not all world-views are religious ones. Remember the seven **dimensions**, or characteristics, of religion?

1. Ritual (regular practices)

2. Experiential (feelings)

3. Story

4. Belief

5. Ethical (right and wrong)

6. Social (community)

7. Material (physical objects, for example buildings)

Actually, they apply to most world-views, **secular** and religious.

Schools in this country, for example, have particular world-views. Below are some examples.

---

1. Ritual: assemblies, the timetable, rules about how to talk to teachers.

2. Experiential: a sense of belonging, pride in achievements.

3. Story: the school prospectus, newspaper articles about the school.

4. Belief: most schools have a charter of values that people share, such as a commitment to success and mutual respect.

5. Ethical: the school rules that describe appropriate behaviour.

6. Social: groupings such as tutor groups, teaching groups, year groups and houses, and after school activities.

7. Material: school uniform, school buildings, equipment and apparatus.

ACTIVITY THREE ·········

Try to outline your own world-view. Use the seven dimensions to describe what is important to you.

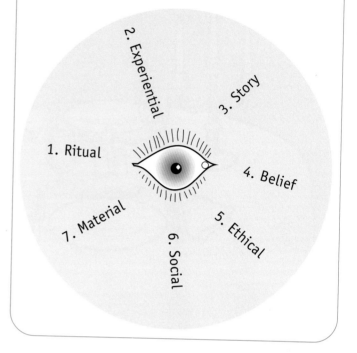

NOW TRY THIS ··············

Interview two people – a friend and a parent, or someone who looks after you – to discover their world-views. Write them up in the seven dimensions, and compare the two. What are the similarities, and what are the differences?

KEY WORDS

Dimension   one of the seven characteristics of a world-view

Secular   non-religious

World-view   the way a person or group of people sees and reacts to the world around them

2. How do beliefs affect people's world-views?

SKILLS

- **matching** beliefs to religions
- **presenting an argument** to provide evidence
- **analysing** statements about religious and secular beliefs
- **reflecting** on your own beliefs about ultimate questions
- **investigating** religious beliefs about ultimate questions

One of the seven dimensions of religions and world-views is *belief*. The kinds of beliefs that affect people's world-views are beliefs about **ultimate questions** of life and death. They might include:

a) What caused the creation of the universe?

b) What is a human being?

c) What happens when a person dies?

d) How do we know what is right and wrong?

e) Is there a purpose to life?

1

I believe that God created everything, including human beings. We were created in His image. He came among us in the body of Jesus Christ to teach us how to live together as human beings. I believe that God has a plan for each of us: each of us has a mission or purpose in life. He reveals it to us, and it is up to us to fulfil it to the best of our ability. Then, when we die, we can have eternal life with God. On the other hand, if we choose to reject Him, we shut the door on Him forever.

2

There is no reason why the universe was created: it just was. Matter – the 'stuff' of the universe – was created from energy. It just happened. In the same way, life came about as a result of chemicals coming together. Human beings are highly evolved life forms. We decide what is good or bad based on what benefits the greatest number of people. It is up to us to find meaning in our lives, and we decide our own fate. And when the body dies, that's the end. Nothing lives on afterwards.

3

We can't really say why the universe exists. But the question is not important. What is important is how to be happy in life. This means overcoming suffering and becoming enlightened to the true nature of life. This is the real aim of life. Life itself is eternal: it has no end. Death is a period of rest between lifetimes. Life is something that we share. We must develop the wisdom to understand this – then we will see that we have to treat all other life forms with compassion and loving-kindness.

4

The Qur'an teaches us that Allah created the universe and everything in it. He created human beings to be different from animals and worship him. He reveals to us in the Holy Qur'an how we should live. We choose how we behave, but Allah knows in advance what we will do. Allah knows all things. After we die, we will have to account to Allah for our actions. He will decide whether we go to Paradise or not.

ACTIVITY TWO ....

Use statements 1, 2, 3 and 4 to decide how a Buddhist, a Christian, a Muslim and a Humanist would answer the five ultimate questions (a–e) below.

ACTIVITY THREE ....

What sort of person might give these answers to the five questions?

a) What caused the creation of the universe?

Don't know; don't care.

b) What is a human being?

An animal with feelings.

c) What happens when a person dies?

Don't know; probably nothing.

d) How do we know what is right and wrong?

If it makes you happy, do it.

e) Is there a purpose to life?

To have fun.

ACTIVITY FOUR ....

How would you answer the five questions?

NOW TRY THIS ....

Find out how a Hindu, Jew or Sikh would answer the five ultimate questions.

KEY WORD

Ultimate questions   important questions concerning what we believe about life

3. What has science got to do with religion?

SKILLS

- **classifying** questions using previous knowledge
- **considering** the benefits of some scientific discoveries
- **explaining** the relationship between science and religion
- **weighing up evidence** to present an argument
- **interpreting** quotations about science and religion

ACTIVITY ONE

1. How was the universe formed?
2. What are human beings made of?
3. Will the universe ever end?
4. What is space?
5. Is there life elsewhere in the universe?
6. Was the universe created?
7. How old is the earth?
8. How did human beings come about?
9. Do humans inherit characteristics from their parents?
10. What is life?

Use your knowledge and understanding of scientific and religious truths to decide which of these questions require science and which require religion to answer them. Remember to give reasons.

In Activity One you may have decided that they are all scientific questions whose answers can be tested empirically (by observing). Yet they are questions that religions have tried to answer. Does this mean that religion and science have the same aims?

ⓘ Are science and religion trying to do the same things?

Science and religion both aim to make sense of the world we live in by looking for patterns in the universe and the things that happen in it. Once we see patterns, we can make predictions about how things will happen. This helps to make our lives better.

For example:

VOLCANOES   If we can find out why volcanoes erupt, then we are better able to predict when they will erupt. Then we can take precautions to minimise the damage they cause.

LIFE   If we can find out why life was created, then we will know what its purpose is. Then we can try to fulfil those aims and live peacefully and happily.

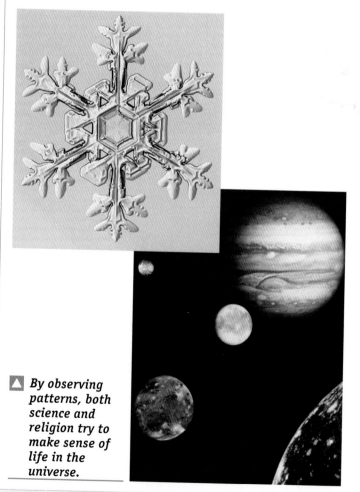

▲ *By observing patterns, both science and religion try to make sense of life in the universe.*

How have humans made sense of the universe?

Some of the first people to observe the universe and investigate how it worked were religious people: Muslims and Christians. They did it for religious reasons.

They started with their religious texts: the Qur'an and the Bible. Both of these books told them that God created the universe. Therefore, by studying the universe, they believed that they could learn more about its creator.

▲ Copernicus (1473–1543) claimed that the earth revolved around the sun. This picture shows the Copernican world system, with the sun at the centre of the universe. Copernicus is pictured in the bottom right-hand corner.

From the eighth to the fourteenth centuries, Muslim scholars investigated astronomy, geography, medicine, chemistry, physics, botany, mathematics and engineering.

From the fifteenth century onwards, European Christians developed those same sciences, and added to them.

The problem came when the things that the new scientists discovered about the universe were different from the things that the Bible and the Christian Church taught.

For example, for a long time the Church taught that the earth was at the centre of the universe, and that everything else moved around it. In 1543, a Polish priest, Nicholas Copernicus, published a book in which he said that the earth travelled around the sun.

Some scientists came to believe that they could explain how the universe works without bringing God into it. In time, religion turned away from trying to explain the physical world. It left that to the scientists. It concentrated on discovering spiritual truths.

ACTIVITY TWO ....

How have human beings used two of the following observations of nature to help improve their lives?

1. The changing seasons.
2. Wood floating on water.
3. Magnets attracting iron.
4. Substances expanding when heated.

ACTIVITY THREE ....

Copernicus was a Christian priest as well as a scientist. His book, which suggested that the earth travelled around the sun (instead of the other way round), was deliberately not published until he was old and dying. Why do you think this was so?

ACTIVITY FOUR ....

Religion has caused many wars throughout history.

Science has found cures for many diseases.

Science is responsible for nuclear weapons.

Religion gives people dignity, self-respect, hope and courage.

Science is responsible for a lot of pollution in the world.

Religion has inspired great works of art.

Religion has inspired terrorism.

Science has enabled us to live lives of luxury.

'Science makes life better; religion makes it worse.'

Do you agree with this opinion? Use the statements above to support your answer. (But remember that not everyone would agree with the statements.)

NOW TRY THIS ....

'The heavens declare the glory of God; the skies proclaim the work of his hands.'

(Psalm 19:1) (Jewish and Christian)

'In the absence of any other proof, the thumb alone would convince me of God's existence.'

(Isaac Newton) (Christian)

'We [i.e. God] made the night dark and gave light to the day, so that you may seek grace from your Lord and learn to work out the seasons and the years. We have made all things absolutely clear to you.'

(Qur'an 17:11–12) (Muslim)

a) What is each of these quotations saying about the purpose of scientific discovery?

b) What is each of these quotations saying about the link between religion and science?

4. Can religion and science agree?

SKILLS

- **comparing** scientific and religious answers to ultimate questions
- **differentiating** between religious and scientific points of view
- **analysing** different points of view
- **discussing** Christian interpretations of the Bible
- **explaining** religious and secular views of scientific observations

ⓘ How do science and religion conflict with each other?

People who say that religion conflicts with science point to three areas of disagreement:

- beliefs about how the universe came into being

- beliefs about how human beings came into existence

- beliefs about what happens to a human being after death.

ACTIVITY ONE ••••••••••••••••••••

Think back to what you have learned about this issue and write down one religious teaching and one scientific belief about each of the three areas of disagreement to show that science and religion appear to disagree.

Do scientists and religious people really disagree with each other? This is a difficult question to answer for a number of reasons.

1. Some scientists are religious, but others are not.
2. Not all scientists agree with each other.
3. Not all religious people agree with each other.

◀ *How did the universe come into being? What does this picture suggest? It is called* **Ancient of Days** *by William Blake, and appeared in his book which was published in 1794.*

ACTIVITY TWO

▲ Richard Dawkins is a British scientist who specialises in zoology. He is also an atheist.

▲ Charles Townes is an American scientist who invented the laser. He is a Christian.

▲ Fay Weldon is a British novelist. She is a Christian.

Which of the people above made the following statements?

QUOTATION A: 'As a scientist, I have been primarily trying to understand our world – the universe (including humans) – what it is and how it works. As a religiously oriented person, I also try to understand the purpose of our universe and human life.'

QUOTATION B: 'Don't expect us to like you [scientists]. You promised us too much and failed to deliver. You never even tried to answer the questions we all asked when we were six. Where did Aunt Maud go when she died? Where was she before she was born?'

QUOTATION C: 'The universe we observe has precisely the properties we should expect. There is, at bottom, no design, no purpose.'

QUOTATION D: 'Science shares with religion the claim that it answers deep questions about origins, the nature of life, and the cosmos (universe). But here the resemblance ends. Scientific beliefs are supported by evidence, and they get results … Faiths are not and do not.'

QUOTATION E: 'Who cares about a second after the Big Bang; what about half a second before? … The scientists just can't face the notion of a variable universe. We can.'

QUOTATION F: 'Science and religion have had a long history of interesting interaction. But … their differences are largely superficial, and … the two become almost indistinguishable if we look at the real nature of each.'

ACTIVITY THREE ·············

1. How would Richard Dawkins, Charles Townes and Fay Weldon answer the following questions?

   a) What are the purposes of science and religion?

   b) Which is more important, and why?

   Use the quotations in Activity Two to support your answer.

2. How would you answer the questions?

ⓘ Does science conflict with religion?

The Jewish, Christian and Muslim scriptures all teach that God created the Universe. They teach, too, that God created all forms of life, including human beings. The biblical story of the creation of the universe in six days is well known, as is the story of the creation of the first man and woman. Not all Christians agree on how to read stories like these.

- Some claim that the Bible, as the word of God, is *literally* true as a matter of historical or scientific fact. The writers of the Bible wrote down what God told them to write, word for word. These people are called **literalists**.

- Some claim that the Bible is a statement of the faith of its writers, who were *inspired* by God. So the Bible was written by human beings, and it reflects the time and culture in which they lived. These people are called **liberals**.

- Some claim that the Bible is the word of God, but its writers *interpreted* some of the messages that God gave to them. So, in some cases they agree with the literalists, and in others they agree with the liberals. These people are called **conservatives**.

ⓘ The Big Bang

The Big Bang theory says that around 13.7 billion years ago the whole of the universe was compressed into the size of a small coin. Scientists call it a singularity. It contained all the energy and matter that was to exist. Apart from the singularity, there was nothing: no space and no time. From the singularity our universe was born through an explosion known as the Big Bang.

After the Big Bang, the energy became atomic particles of helium, hydrogen and lithium. Gravity brought clumps of matter together. The clumps were pulled towards other clumps and eventually formed galaxies. They were thrown away from the centre of the explosion at great speed. The universe is still expanding today.

ACTIVITY FOUR ·············

Can a Christian believe in the Big Bang theory and evolution? Discuss this question with a partner.

NOW TRY THIS ·············

Imagine two scientists, one an atheist and one a Christian, discussing the relationship between science and religion on a television show. Write a script of their discussion. Try to include their thoughts about:

- whether the universe has a purpose

- what differences science makes to people's lives

- what differences religion makes to people's lives

- different ways of interpreting scripture.

KEY WORDS

Atheist   a person who does not believe in a God

Conservative   a person who believes that the Bible is the word of God, but has been interpreted by human beings

Liberal   a person who believes that the Bible was inspired by God, but is not to be taken as scientific fact

Literalist   a person who believes that the Bible is literally and scientifically true

5. Can religion make sense of the world?

SKILLS

- **interpreting** an allegory
- **reflecting** on the hypothesis that everything has a purpose
- **applying** beliefs about the purpose of life to behaviour in daily life
- **analysing** religious views about the purpose of life
- **comparing** religious views

An allegory

Read the following story:

Once upon a time, two explorers came upon a clearing in the jungle. In the clearing there were many flowers and many weeds growing. One explorer said, 'Some gardener must tend this plot.' The other disagreed, 'There is no gardener.' So they pitched their tents and set a watch. No gardener is seen. 'But perhaps he is an invisible gardener.' So they set up a barbed-wire fence. They electrify it. They patrol with bloodhounds. (For they remember how H. G. Wells's The Invisible Man *could be both smelt and touched, though he could not be seen.) But no shrieks ever suggest that some intruder has received a shock. No movements of the wire ever betray an invisible climber. The bloodhounds never give cry. Yet still the believer is convinced. 'But there is a gardener, unable to be seen or touched, who does not feel electric shocks. A gardener who has no scent and makes no sound, a gardener who comes secretly to look after the garden which he loves.' At last the non-believer despairs, 'But what remains of your original claim? Just how does what you call an invisible, untouchable, eternally-mysterious gardener differ from an imaginary gardener, or even from no gardener at all?'*

ACTIVITY ONE ················

1. In the story, what does the garden represent?

2. What does the gardener represent?

3. What does the explorer who believes in the gardener represent?

4. What does the explorer who does not believe in the gardener represent?

5. Explain the meaning of the story in your own words.

6. Do you think that this is a good allegory? Give reasons for your answer.

This kind of story is called an **allegory**. An allegory is a story that so closely resembles some aspects of life that we can learn about life from it. This one was told by philosopher, John Wisdom. One of the points he was making is that most religious and non-religious people do not disagree about the empirical facts of the universe, but that they react to them in different ways. In other words, they have different world-views. Neither is able to prove whether they are right or wrong.

ACTIVITY TWO ·····································

Discuss the following questions with a partner.
What is the point of:

- playing video games

- going to school

- keeping a pet

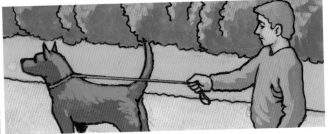

- wearing a tie

- reading a book?

Everything we do has a purpose. Religious people believe that living is no exception. You could say that religion is the attempt to find meaning and purpose in life, and then to fulfil it.

ACTIVITY THREE ·············

If someone believed that the only purpose of their life was to become as wealthy as possible, they may be dishonest in their dealings with others. They may be mean, they may be ambitious, and they may become big headed.

You may already have thought about what purpose your life has. How does this affect you as a person and the way you live your life?

ACTIVITY FOUR ················

Read carefully the statements below about the purpose of life.

a) Which *two* purposes do all six of these religions share?

b) How might these beliefs affect the way people live their lives?

NOW TRY THIS ·············

a) Why does Buddhism have a different teaching about the purpose of life from the religions below?

b) What is the purpose of life, according to Buddhism?

Christianity

Jesus said in the Bible: "Love the Lord your God with all your heart and with all your soul and with all your mind and with all your strength … Love your neighbour as yourself." (Mark 12:30–31) This is our goal in life.'

Islam

'Allah says in the Qur'an: "I have created … human beings only so that they may worship me. I do not require support from them, nor that they should feed me." (Surah 51:56–57) Those who truly worship Allah will be full of love and affection for their brothers and sisters in humanity.'

Baha'i

'The main purpose of life for Baha'i is to know and love God. Baha'i texts say that work performed in the spirit of service to humanity is a form of worship.'

Judaism

'God is the source of all existence. In Judaism, life is valued above all else. All people are descended from a single person, so taking a single life is like destroying an entire world, and saving a single life is like saving an entire world.'

Hinduism

'Life's main purpose is to discover the spiritual nature and the peace and fulfilment it brings for all beings.'

Sikhism

'Sikhs believe the purpose of life is to find union with God by following the teachings of the Gurus and respecting the oneness of the human race.'

6. How does religion make sense of the world?

SKILLS

* **analysing** quotations from religious texts on the value of human life
* **speculating** on secular arguments to support the idea that human life is special
* **formulating** religious responses to moral issues
* **expressing** ideas symbolically
* **evaluating** a moral statement

ⓘ What is the sanctity of life?

Religious people talk about the sanctity of life, or speak about life being sacred. They mean that human life is special in a religious way and for religious reasons.

Of course, (almost) everyone believes that human life is special and worthy of the highest respect, but only religious people use the word 'sacred'.

Read the quotations from six religions, below and on the following page, to get an idea of their thoughts on the value of human life.

Islam

'Do not kill or take human life which God has declared to be sacred.'

(Qur'an Surah 6:151)

Judaism and Christianity

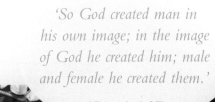

'So God created man in his own image; in the image of God he created him; male and female he created them.'

(Genesis 1:27)

'"Before I formed you in the womb I knew you, before you were born I set you apart".'

(Jeremiah 1:5)

'"You gave me life and showed me kindness".'

(Job 10:12)

Buddhism

'It is rare good fortune
to be born as a human being.'

(Sayings of the Buddha in
Forty-two Sections 36)

'Life is the most precious
of all treasures. Even one extra
day of life is worth more than
ten million coins of gold.'

(Nichiren [Buddhist teacher],
On Prolonging One's Lifespan)

Hinduism

Sikhism

'Don't you know
that your life is decreasing,
day and night? … That body,
which you believe to be your own,
and your beautiful home and spouse,
none of these is yours to keep.'

(Guru Granth Sahib 220)

'All this is Brahman (God) …
He is my self within the heart, smaller than
a corn of rice, smaller than a corn of barley,
smaller than a mustard seed, smaller than a
canary seed or the kernel of a canary seed. He is
also myself within the heart, greater than the
earth, greater than the sky, greater than heaven,
greater than all these worlds.'

(Khândogya Upanishad 3.14:1–3)

ACTIVITY ONE ● ● ● ● ● ● ● ● ● ● ● ●

Having read the quotations from the six religions,
what reasons do you think religious people have for
saying that human life is sacred?

ACTIVITY TWO ● ● ● ● ● ● ● ● ● ● ● ●

What reasons might a non-religious person have for
believing that human life is uniquely special?

Think about the reasons why human life is protected
in law, why adults care for children, why the elderly
are cared for, why doctors try to help people to live
long lives, and why some people are kept on life-
support machines.

Discuss your ideas with a partner.

ⓘ Defining terms

abortion (NOUN) an operation or other intervention to end a pregnancy by removing an embryo or foetus from the womb

suicide (NOUN) the act of deliberately killing yourself

euthanasia (NOUN) the act or practice of killing somebody who has an incurable illness or injury, or allowing or assisting that person to die

ACTIVITY THREE ....

1. Based on their belief in the sanctity of life, what views are different religious people likely to have about:

   a) abortion

   b) suicide

   c) euthanasia?

2. What are your views on these issues? Remember: you must give reasons for all of your answers.

NOW TRY THIS ....

'Some human beings are kept alive against their will, without dignity, and in extreme pain, in conditions that would be illegal in the case of an animal.'

a) How would someone who believed in the sanctity of life respond to this statement?

b) How do you respond to it?

ACTIVITY FOUR ....

You can see below three examples of logos of non-religious charities. They are using symbols to get across the idea that human life is precious.

Design a symbol that represents religious ideas about the sanctity of life.

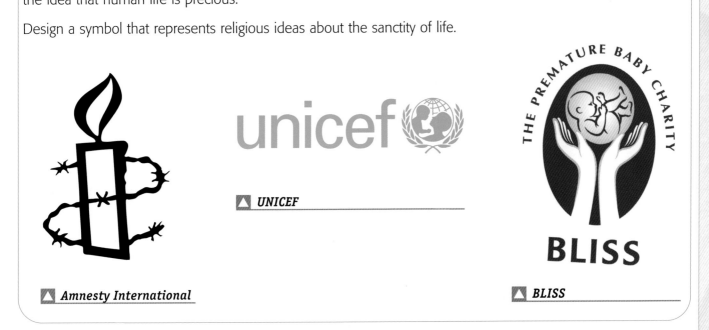

▲ Amnesty International

▲ UNICEF

▲ BLISS

SUMMARY OF UNIT 2

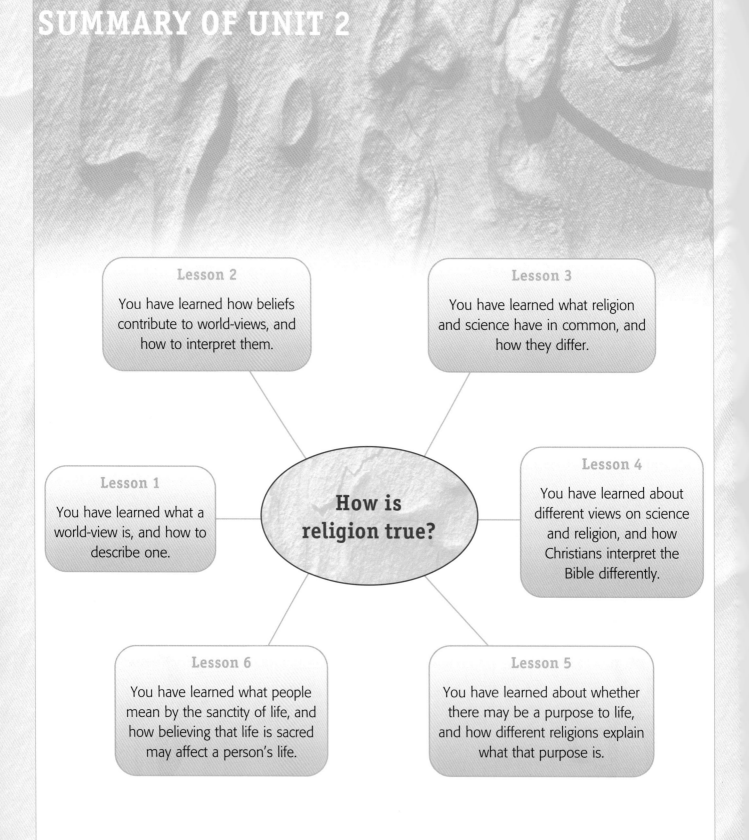

Lesson 2

You have learned how beliefs contribute to world-views, and how to interpret them.

Lesson 3

You have learned what religion and science have in common, and how they differ.

Lesson 1

You have learned what a world-view is, and how to describe one.

How is religion true?

Lesson 4

You have learned about different views on science and religion, and how Christians interpret the Bible differently.

Lesson 6

You have learned what people mean by the sanctity of life, and how believing that life is sacred may affect a person's life.

Lesson 5

You have learned about whether there may be a purpose to life, and how different religions explain what that purpose is.

UNIT 3: WHERE DOES THE EVIDENCE COME FROM?

Lesson 1: What is authority?

◎ Read about different meanings of the word 'authority'.

◎ Find out where authority comes from.

◎ Where does religious authority come from, and how is it used?

Lesson 2: Why do people form communities?

◎ Discuss how people form and belong to communities.

◎ Discover how communities contribute to world-views.

◎ Learn about religious communities.

◎ Create charts to represent the numbers of religious believers in the world and the UK.

◎ Design a poster illustrating the information gained in the lesson.

Lesson 3: What do religious leaders do?

◎ Review the nature of leadership.

◎ Identify how religious leaders see themselves.

◎ Form your own opinion on the qualities a religious leader should have, and why they would want to become a leader.

Lesson 4: Why is tradition important?

◎ Think about how world-views are passed on from one generation to the next.

◎ Discover how festivals pass on religious teachings.

◎ Identify how symbols are used in religious festivals.

◎ Discuss any other purposes for religious festivals.

Lesson 5: What authority do religious texts have?

◎ Discuss the idea that books can be sources of authority.

◎ Learn about some religious books by extracting information from a passage and creating a table.

◎ Find out how religious books are treated and suggest why.

Lesson 6: How do religious people learn about their faith?

◎ Think about how religious authorities are used to pass on faith.

◎ Conduct an investigation to gather information about how people learn about their religion.

◎ Communicate the information you gather in a © *PowerPoint presentation graphics programme*.

1. What is authority?

SKILLS

- **thinking about** what authority means
- **analysing** the authority you have, and the authority others have over you
- **identifying** different types of authority, including religious authority
- **classifying** types of authority

Discuss these questions with a partner.

1. What do you understand by the word 'authority'?
2. Who has authority in your life? Draw a spider diagram with yourself at the centre, and those with authority around you. What authority does each of them have over you?

ⓘ How do we use the word 'authority'?

- We have seen that authority can mean power, or the right to power. When we say that parents, teachers, judges or the police have authority over us, we mean that they are entitled to have some sort of control over our lives.

- It can also mean a source of knowledge or wisdom. For example, when we say, 'Professor Brain is an authority on the English Civil War,' we mean that the professor is an expert whose opinion can be trusted.

  These two meanings are connected. Very often, people who have special knowledge or wisdom, and are trustworthy, also have power.

▶ *What power does a referee have? What special knowledge does he have?*

ACTIVITY TWO ·················

Jade is thirteen years old. She has a brother who is eight, and a sister who is six. In the mornings, she helps to get them ready for school. At her own school, she represents her tutor group on the school council. She also helps with organising lunches at the junior school next door.

In the evenings, she takes her dog, Charlie, for a walk, and feeds him and her pet guinea pig, Boris. On Fridays, Jade goes to Guides, where she is a Patrol Leader.

Jade holds many positions of authority. Discuss what they are with your partner and then answer the questions below.

1. What positions of authority do you hold?
2. What powers do you have?
3. Where does your authority come from?
4. What qualifies you to have this authority?

ⓘ Where does authority come from?

If we want to know something, we go to an authority. This could be:

- A book or some other part of the information media, such as the Internet.

- A person: a teacher or some other expert.

- Tradition: knowledge is handed down from generation to generation.

- The community we live in: people who share our world-view.

ACTIVITY THREE ··············

1. How many different sources of authority can you spot in the picture below?
2. What authority do they have?

ⓘ What are the *religious* sources of authority?

The major religions of the world have their own sources of authority. They provide guidance and wisdom that people trust to help them with their lives. These sources of authority include:

- Books: most religions have a special book or books. They are often called scriptures.

- Person: most religions have leaders or teachers.

- Tradition: religious teachings are passed on through the generations.

- Community: members of religious groups support each other.

For religious people, these forms of authority form part of the evidence that persuades them that their religion is true. In this unit you will examine each of these forms of authority in greater detail.

ACTIVITY FOUR

1. Write a list of the sources of authority in your school.

2. Which of the different sorts of authority does each source have?

3. Where does the authority come from?

NOW TRY THIS

Authority has to be given to a person or a thing.

a) Where might the Queen get her authority from?

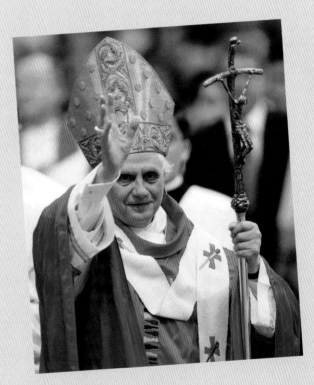

b) Where might religious authorities and leaders get their authority from?

2. Why do people form communities?

SKILLS

• **explaining** why you belong to groups
• **thinking about** how the groups you belong to contribute to your world-view
• **explaining** the link between religion and community
• **drawing charts** to show the number of followers of different religions
• **expressing** information in the form of a poster

After completing Activity One, you will probably discover that you belong to a number of different groups. Some of them you chose to join: friendship groups, sports clubs, music groups. Some of them you had no choice about: your family, your tutor group, your neighbourhood.

Yet all of these groups help you to form your world-view. They make you the person you are.

ACTIVITY ONE

1. Write a list of groups that you are part of or belong to, for example, a group of friends, a school club, or a football team.
2. What is the purpose of each of them?
3. Which of these groups did you choose to join?
4. Why did you choose to join them?

ACTIVITY TWO ....

1. How do the following groups contribute to your world-view:
   - your family
   - your friends
   - your school?

2. What do you contribute to the groups you belong to?

ⓘ Why do humans form groups?

There are many reasons why humans form groups. Here are some of them:

- to share a world-view
- to pass on a world-view
- to learn a world-view
- to help and support other members.

  Can you think of any other reasons?

ACTIVITY THREE ....

1. What is the meaning of the word 'religion'? (Remember: the 'lig' bit of the word comes from the same root as the 'lig' in the word 'ligament'.)
2. What has this got to do with 'community'?

ⓘ Religious communities

People who share religious world-views usually form groups or communities. People may be born into a religious community, or may choose to join one. Here are some examples. (Words in bold are explained in the Glossary at the end of the book.)

Christianity

The worldwide community of Christians is called the **Church**. It is estimated that there are about 2,000 million Christians throughout the world, about 41 million of whom live in Britain.

Christians broadly share the same beliefs: that God created the universe, that he took human form as Jesus Christ, and that he lives on in the hearts of human beings. But they do not all agree on everything. So the Christian Church is subdivided into smaller groups, called **denominations**. The Roman Catholic Church and the Church of England are two examples.

You join most denominations by being **baptised** into them. If this happens when you are a baby, you have a chance to confirm your decision when you are older, at a ceremony called **confirmation**.

Sikhism

The central Sikh community is known as the **Khalsa** (the Pure Community, or brotherhood and sisterhood of Sikhs), though not all Sikhs become members. There are roughly 23 million Sikhs in the world, of which about 335,000 live in Britain.

There is a great emphasis in Sikhism on equality and unity, so all Sikhs have the same status and there are no divisions between them. To become a member of the Khalsa, Sikhs go through a ceremony called **Amrit Sanskar**. They promise to worship one God, follow Sikh ethical teaching and serve other people. They also wear the **Five Ks**, the Sikh uniform.

Islam

The community of Muslims is called the **Ummah**, which means brotherhood or family. There are thought to be about 1,300 million Muslims in the world, and about 1.6 million in Britain.

All Muslims follow the teachings of the Qur'an as the word of God. However, a disagreement about who was to be **Caliph** (leader of the Muslims) led to the division of the Ummah into two groups: the **Sunni** and the **Shi'ah**. Today, about 80 per cent of Muslims are Sunni, and there is no overall Muslim leader.

In order to be a Muslim, you must believe and declare that Allah is the only God, and that Muhammad is his **prophet** (messenger).

Buddhism

The Buddhist community is called the **Sangha**, which means 'assembly'. About 380 million people practise Buddhism in the world, though only about 150,000 of them live in Britain.

All Buddhists try to follow the teachings of Siddhartha Gautama (the **Buddha**), though there are slight differences in the ways they do it. There are three main schools of Buddhism: Theravada, Mahayana and Vajrayana. The Mahayana school is further subdivided into smaller groups, or **sects**.

There are no rules in Buddhism, so there are no regulations about what counts as a Buddhist. However, a person who follows the Buddha's teachings (the **Dharma**) is generally called a Buddhist.

Hinduism

Hinduism is a word used to describe a huge number of religious practices that started in India thousands of years ago. There are about 900 million Hindus in the world, and about 560,000 live in Britain.

There is no single community of Hindus. Those who practise Hinduism share a belief that God (**Brahman**) is everything, and everything is God. Different Hindu groups concentrate their worship on different aspects of God. ISKCON (The International Society for Krishna Consciousness) has become popular over the last 40 years.

Judaism

Jews are people who are born Jewish. A person is a Jew if his or her mother is Jewish. So a person can be Jewish even if he or she is not religious.

Religious Jews believe in one God who established an agreement with the Jewish people, that he would protect them and they should obey him. **Orthodox** (strict) Jews are those who believe that the laws laid down in the **Torah** (part of the Jewish Bible) should be followed exactly. **Progressive** (liberal) Jews believe that these laws may be adapted for the modern world. There are roughly 14 million Jews in the world, including 267,000 in Britain. The sign of belonging to the Jewish community is, for males, **circumcision** (the removal of the foreskin of the penis). This happens when the baby boy is eight days old.

ACTIVITY FOUR ....

1. Draw a bar chart to show the numbers of followers of the major religions in the world.

2. Draw a bar chart to show the numbers of followers of the major religions in Britain.

3. Compare the two charts. What is the same? What is different? Is there anything that surprises you?

NOW TRY THIS ....

Using the information on this page, design a poster to show *either* the divisions within religions, *or* signs of belonging to a religion. Try to find some photographs to illustrate it.

3. What do religious leaders do?

SKILLS

- **identifying** the different roles that leaders have
- **describing** the role of a leader of one religion
- **comparing** the roles of different religious leaders
- **explaining** why people become religious leaders

ACTIVITY ONE

These pictures all show people who have influence in their communities. Make a list of the things they do for the people of their communities. Who else can you add to the list? What do they do?

▶ *Doctor*

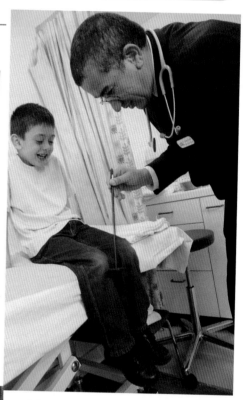

▲ *Conductor of an orchestra*

▲ *Captain of a football team*

▲ *Teacher*

▲ *MP in Parliament*

▲ *Bank manager*

Below and on the following page are descriptions of six religious leaders and their roles within their religions and communities.

Different Christian denominations have different names for their leaders. I am a **priest** in the Church of England. I see my job as leading people to an understanding of the presence of God in their lives. I am a leader in the community who works together with people to proclaim God's promise of hope, life and justice. I welcome new life into the community through Baptism, and I witness the promise of love through the commitment of marriage, and the beginning of family life. I visit the sick and those who are troubled. I preach the good news about Jesus and try to get people to carry it into their lives. I wear a clerical collar as a symbol of my priesthood.

I am a **rabbi**, a leader in the Jewish community. People think of a rabbi as someone who conducts ceremonies and funerals, but we are much more than that. The word 'rabbi' means 'teacher'. The ideal rabbi is a scholar of the Bible who guides the members of the community he serves. How do I know how to guide them correctly? I turn to the Torah and Judaism for answers. One of the rabbi's primary roles is to answer questions that members of his community may have about everyday behaviour, so that it is in accordance with Jewish law. I also serve as a counsellor, giving members of the community advice and guidance on every subject under the sun, from marriage and raising children to business ethics. Finally, my job is to inspire community members to become better people. I try to do this both through individual example and by sharing the knowledge I have obtained by becoming a Torah scholar.

There are many different kinds of Buddhist monks, just as there are many different types of Buddhism. I am a **bhikkhu**, a monk of the Theravada school. Our daily life follows a strict schedule, and each monk's life revolves around meditation, the study of scriptures, and the taking part in ceremonies. Daily life involves interaction with the community and with my fellow bhikkhus. I live and work in a temple, but I am occasionally involved in community affairs, such as participating in Buddhist festivals. I sometimes get involved in the blessing of new homes or businesses, and also in the teaching of trainee monks, short-term monks, or the community. A temple monk's **pastoral** activity is a transaction between monks and householders; this is where a monk passes spiritual blessings to the community. In return, the community offers food, money, and other everyday items. Monks do not have to make a lifetime commitment, so some choose to only wear the robe for a few months, weeks or days, and then there are some that choose to dedicate their entire life to Buddha.

I am an **imam**.
The word 'imam' means 'one who leads', and it is my job to lead the community in prayer and worship. I don't have any special training to be an imam, but I have studied Islam and the Qur'an. It is because of this that I was chosen by my local community to be their leader. Apart from leading the prayers, I preach the Friday sermon. I teach about Islam to people of all ages, especially to the children who need to learn to read the Qur'an in the original Arabic. I organise many other things, such as educational programmes at the mosque. I visit many schools in the area, and speak to many non-Muslim groups. I am also an authorised Muslim prison and hospital chaplain.

In the Sikh faith, the **Guru Granth Sahib**, our holy book, is our leader. It is the central focus of every service of worship. While in its presence, Sikhs must remove their shoes and cover their heads out of respect. I am a **granthi**: I lead the worship because I have a greater understanding of the book, but I am not thought of as above the other people. This is consistent with the Sikh ideals of unity and equality. In worship services, the Guru Granth Sahib is placed on a pedestal of pillows, and is opened and closed ceremoniously. It is transported with the utmost care. Some Sikhs may have a copy of the Guru Granth Sahib in their homes, but they give it a room of its own and create a platform of pillows and beautiful cloths on which to place it. Most Sikhs read the Guru Granth Sahib every day and meditate upon it. It is frequently read from cover to cover as a method of prayer or thanksgiving.

I am a **swami**.
The word 'swami' means 'master': it means working to be master of your own life, so that the life that is God may come shining through. Becoming a swami is not so much adding something to your life, as it is an act of setting aside. A swami is one who has set aside all of the limited, worldly pursuits, so as to devote full-time effort to the direct experience of the highest spiritual realisation, and to the service of enabling others to do the same. A swami who has perfected this state may be called a **guru**. In India, most villages have a guru. The guru teaches and serves others. Some of those who hear his teachings become his disciples (followers), and they pass his teachings on to others.

ACTIVITY TWO ....

Using the information, write a description of the role of *one* religious leader in his or her community.

ACTIVITY THREE ....

Compare your description of a religious leader with other people's descriptions of other religious leaders. What do they have in common?

NOW TRY THIS ....

Why might a person want to become a religious leader? Write a list of as many reasons as you can.

4. Why is tradition important?

SKILLS

- **thinking about** ways in which traditions are passed on
- **identifying** features of religious festivals
- **representing in symbols** different aspects of a religious festival
- **reflecting** on reasons why people celebrate, and how they feel

ⓘ What does tradition mean?

The word 'tradition' comes from two Latin words which mean 'to give over'. When we talk about tradition, we mean the ways we pass on world-views, including religious world-views, from one generation to the next.

ⓘ Religious festivals

If you want to make sure that you remember something accurately, you have to keep going over it at regular intervals. If you learned a poem by heart, or the words of a song, and did nothing more, the chances are you would forget it within a couple of weeks. You would need to repeat it to yourself fairly frequently to keep it fresh in your mind – just like you do when you revise for a test!

One way that religions remember and pass on important stories and teachings is through regular participation in festivals. On the following pages are some examples of religious festivals and photos which illustrate them.

ACTIVITY ONE ....

How could you pass on details about you and your life so that your great-great-grandchildren would know you as well as your brother or sister might? What information would you want to pass on? How would you do it? How could you make sure that the information was passed on accurately?

What was he really like?

KEY WORDS

Baisakhi   Sikh festival to mark the founding of the Khalsa

Divali   Hindu festival of lights

Easter   Christian festival that commemorates the Resurrection of Jesus

Enlightenment   the state of being enlightened

Id-ul-Fitr   Islamic festival to mark the end of Ramadan

Pesach   Jewish festival to commemorate the freedom of the ancient Jewish people from slavery

Ramadan   Islamic month of fasting

Resurrection   a rising of the dead (usually refers to Jesus Christ)

Seder   a special meal held during the Jewish festival of Pesach

Wesak   Buddhist festival to remember the birth, death and enlightenment of the Buddha

Hinduism

An ancient Hindu story tells of a prince called Rama who risked his life in a daring battle to save his wife, Sita. It is a story of the triumph of good over evil. Hindus celebrate the story and what it teaches them in a festival called **Divali**.
Divali means 'lights', and Hindus decorate their homes and public buildings with lights. It happens at the time of the Hindu New Year, so people make sure that their business affairs are up to date and their houses are clean and bright.

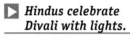
▶ *Hindus celebrate Divali with lights.*

Buddhism

Buddhists celebrate the life of Siddhartha Gautama, the Buddha, with a festival called **Wesak**. Siddhartha is said to have discovered the true meaning of life. This is called **enlightenment**. It is represented at the festival by light: people carry lanterns through the streets, illuminated floats process through towns and cities, and houses are lit up. It shows the belief that the teachings of the Buddha are able to brighten the darkness that exists in everyone's life. People wash statues of the Buddha.

▲ *Wesak is a festival of light.*

Islam

Muhammad first received the Qur'an during **Ramadan**, the ninth month of the Islamic calendar. During the daylight hours of Ramadan, Muslims neither eat nor drink. This is to develop self-control and overcome selfishness. **Id-ul-Fitr** is a festival to mark the end of the month of Ramadan. Muslims say special prayers at the Mosque to thank Allah for his blessings. They give each other cards and presents and have a big feast.

▲ *Id-ul-Fitr is a time of celebration for Muslims.*

Christianity

The most important belief in the Christian faith is the belief in the **Resurrection**. The Bible says that, three days after he was killed, Jesus came back to life again. Christians believe that, when Jesus died, the sins

▲ *Churches are brightly decorated at Easter time.*

of human beings died with him. Christians believe that when Jesus came back to life, he enabled all people to make a new start in their relationship with God. The Resurrection represents the triumph of God over evil, of life over death. It offers hope.

Christians remember the Resurrection and teachings about it at **Easter** time. Churches are decorated with gold and silver ornaments, and white and yellow spring flowers. They echo with the noise of singing and of bells ringing. They are filled with light.

Judaism

About 4,000 years ago, the Jewish people were kept as slaves in a foreign land. One of them, Moses, tried to secure their freedom, but negotiations were unsuccessful. The Bible says that God punished the Jews' captors in ten ways before they freed them: the Ten Plagues.

Jews remember this event in a festival called **Pesach** (Passover). During this time Jews have a special meal, called the **Seder**. They light candles, and have foods that represent various aspects of the story, such as lamb, eggs and green vegetables. The festival is a celebration of the freedom God brought to them.

◀ *Jews use food symbolically at Pesach.*

Sikhism

In 1699, the Khalsa was founded by Guru Gobind Singh, the tenth leader of the Sikhs. This happened on the day of **Baisakhi**, the Sikh New Year. At this time, he appointed the Guru Granth Sahib, the holy book, to guide the Sikhs after him. Sikhs celebrate this by reading the Granth all the way through. They take down the Sikh flag, wash down the flagpole, and fly a new flag. This is traditionally the time when people join the Khalsa and become full members of the Sikh faith.

▲ *Sikhs replace their flag at Baisakhi.*

ACTIVITY TWO

1. Which festivals have symbols of the hope of new life?
2. What are those symbols?
3. Which festivals use light as a symbol?
4. What does light symbolise?

ACTIVITY THREE

1. It is common at festivals for people to have a meal together. Why do you think this is so?
2. Design a card inviting someone to a meal to celebrate one of the festivals described above. Use colour and symbols rather than drawing pictures to represent the things that the festival commemorates.

ACTIVITY FOUR

Think about festivals and other times when you celebrate. What do you like best about these occasions, and why?

Pool your ideas with the rest of the class. Can you come up with your top ten reasons to celebrate?

NOW TRY THIS

a) What purposes do celebrations have, other than handing down beliefs and teachings? Give some examples.

b) What feelings and emotions do you associate with each of these purposes?

5. What authority do religious texts have?

SKILLS

- **expressing** your thoughts and feelings about a book you have enjoyed
- **extracting** information from text
- **explaining** the authority of holy books
- **suggesting** ways in which people might put their respect for holy books into practice

Human beings have always recognised the importance of recording important parts of their lives. Before people had alphabets to write down words, they drew pictures of great events.

Once they were able to write down the words they spoke, they were able to describe not only events, but also the things that people said, and even thought.

The authority that a piece of writing has depends on:

- who wrote it
- the number of people that read it
- the influence or effect it has on them
- the length of time it has been in circulation.

ACTIVITY ONE

Think about a book that you have enjoyed. Write a short review of it explaining who wrote it, when it was published (i.e. is it new or old?), what you enjoyed about it, how popular it is, how the writer held your interest, and what effect it had on you. What authority do you think the book has?

Each of the major religions has its own special or holy book, which followers think has great authority. This section contains some facts about them.

ⓘ What are the holy books?

The holy books of most religions go back for thousands of years. Some of the oldest are the **Vedas**, texts that are special to Hindus. They were put together between 1000 and 500 BCE.

▶ *Some Hindu scriptures are highly decorated.*

During the same time period, the Jewish Bible, the **Tenakh**, was compiled.

◀ *A Jewish man reads the Torah using a yad.*

Since Jesus was Jewish, the Tenakh was his holy book, and so is included in the Christian **Bible**. Christians call it the Old Testament. The New Testament of the Christian Bible tells the story of Jesus and what happened to his followers after his death and resurrection. It also contains the teachings of Jesus and his followers. It was written in the first century CE.

▶ *A Bible is placed on a lectern, where it is read from during a service.*

The Buddhist scriptures were put together in the first century BCE. Buddhists have many special writings, but the most commonly used are called the **Tipitaka**. They contain stories about the Buddha, and details about his teachings. They also contain rules for Buddhist monks.

▲ *The Tipitaka.*

The **Qur'an**, the book that is special to Muslims, was taught by the prophet, Muhammad, during the first half of the seventh century. It was compiled in about 650 CE.

Some Islamic, and also Hindu, writings were included in the Adi Granth, the Sikh book that was compiled in 1604 CE. More Sikh writings were added in 1706 CE, and the Adi Granth became the **Guru Granth Sahib**, the eleventh Sikh guru.

Religious writings pass on religious and ethical teachings and encourage their readers in their lives. In the New Testament of the Christian Bible, for example, the Gospels (the accounts of Jesus' life) are stories in which Jesus delivers his teachings. Yet most of the New Testament consists of letters written by the early Christians to explain the teachings. Christians believe that it was inspired by God.

▲ *The Qur'an wrapped in a protective cloth.*

▲ *The Guru Granth Sahib is kept in a special area of the Gurdwara and is carried out during a service.*

The Jewish Bible contains the teachings and commandments given to the Jewish people by God, prophecy (messages from God), poems and hymns. The Qur'an consists entirely of prophecies, and so Muslims believe that its words are actually the words of God. The Sikh holy book, the Guru Granth Sahib, comprises hymns and prayers to God, as do many of the Hindu scriptures. Some Hindu writings take the form of stories and myths.

ACTIVITY TWO ●

Carefully read the information on the previous pages about holy books. There are a lot of facts about Buddhist, Christian, Hindu, Islamic, Jewish and Sikh scriptures. Use this information to compile a data bank for each religion. You could put the information into a table, as below.

Name of religion	Date of compilation	Contents
Buddhism		
Christianity		
Hinduism		
Islam		
Judaism		
Sikhism		

ACTIVITY THREE ● ● ● ● ● ● ● ● ● ● ● ● ●

Write a paragraph to explain what authority the holy books have. You will need to think about when and why they were written, the kind of information they contain, and who wrote them.

ACTIVITY FOUR ● ● ● ● ● ● ● ● ● ● ● ● ● ●

Religious people treat their holy books with great respect.

1. Give reasons why they do so.
2. Suggest ways in which holy books might be treated to show respect for them. Use the photographs on the previous pages to help you.

NOW TRY THIS ● ● ● ● ● ● ● ● ● ● ● ●

Christians, Jews and Muslims are sometimes called 'the People of the Book'. Why might this be so?

KEY WORDS

Bible the Christian holy book
Guru Granth Sahib the Sikh holy book
Qur'an the holy book of Islam
Tenakh the Jewish holy book, sometimes called the Bible
Tipitaka the collection of Buddhist holy scriptures
Vedas the oldest of the Hindu holy books

6. How do religious people learn about their faith?

SKILLS

- **recalling** information from previous lessons
- **thinking about** the sources of beliefs and values
- **explaining** how religious beliefs and practices are passed from generation to generation
- **presenting** information using © *PowerPoint*

In this unit, we have looked at the various ways in which people from different faiths learn about their religion, and how information is passed on. This lesson consolidates what you have learned in the form of an imaginary interview and a © *PowerPoint* presentation. Below is what the first slide of your presentation could look like. Read the following page to find out your task for the lesson.

Keeping the faith

ACTIVITY ••

Task

You are a television producer. You have been asked by a major television company to make a documentary to be called *Keeping the Faith*. It is about how people learn about their religion. Before the television company gives you the contract, they want to know what you will put in your programme. Your task is to design a © *PowerPoint* presentation to give to their board of directors outlining the content of your programme.

Guidelines

In the last five lessons, you have learned about the ways in which religion is passed from generation to generation. You have learned about the part that religious communities play in this; the role of religious leaders; how religious festivals pass on religious teachings; and how holy books teach the faiths. You will need to draw on this information.

First of all, you will need to choose one of the six religions you have learned about: Buddhism, Christianity, Hinduism, Islam, Judaism or Sikhism. You will then need to think about how to present the information.

Most documentary films combine a voice-over commentary with interviews. In this way, they get their information across. So, in your first © *PowerPoint* slide you should try to answer the question, 'What influences me in my beliefs and values?' Then you could write up an interview with an imaginary person to show how they learn about their faith. You should ask them about how their religious community supports them; about their beliefs concerning their holy book; about the role of the leader of their community; and about how traditions teach aspects of their faith. Each slide of your presentation should show one question and the answer. Below and opposite are some examples of questions you could ask.

NOW TRY THIS ....

Conduct a second interview with a member of a different faith to the first one you chose. Emphasise some of the differences between this and your first interview, as well as the similarities. Give reasons for the differences.

SUMMARY OF UNIT 3

Lesson 2

You have learned about why people form communities, and how they form them.

Lesson 3

You have learned about the role of a leader, and why people become religious leaders.

Lesson 1

You have learned about what authority is, and where religious authority comes from.

Where does the evidence come from?

Lesson 4

You have learned about how festivals pass on religious teachings, and how symbols are used.

Lesson 6

You have learned about how religious beliefs and practices are passed on, how to carry out an imaginary interview and how to present this information in a © PowerPoint presentation.

Lesson 5

You have learned about why some books are special in some religions, and how people's respect for them is shown in the ways they treat them.

UNIT 4: HOW IS RELIGIOUS AUTHORITY USED?

Lesson 1: How are Jewish scriptures used?

◎ Find out about the composition of the Jewish scriptures.

◎ Interpret the Jewish scriptures.

◎ Evaluate the Jewish scriptures.

◎ Learn about aspects of Jewish life.

◎ Discover how the Jewish scriptures are used in worship.

◎ Decide for yourself why you think the scriptures are important for Jews.

Lesson 2: What does the Bible teach Christians about God?

◎ Find out about Jewish and Christian ideas about the messiah.

◎ Understand what a parable is.

◎ Try interpreting a parable.

◎ Identify what Christians understand about the Kingdom of God.

◎ Experiment with writing your own parable.

Lesson 3: How do the Buddhist scriptures guide people's lives?

◎ Learn how the Buddha taught.

◎ Find out about the composition of the Buddhist scriptures.

◎ Interpret some Buddhist teachings.

◎ Evaluate some Buddhist teachings.

◎ Identify and understand Buddhist symbols and create a poster using them.

Lesson 4: What are the Hindu scriptures about?

◎ Find out about the composition of the Hindu scriptures.

◎ Discover the Hindu idea of the soul.

◎ Interpret the Hindu scriptures.

◎ Learn how to symbolise Hindu values.

Lesson 5: What does the Qur'an tell us about Islamic beliefs?

◎ Understand the basic beliefs of Islam.

◎ Consider how Islamic beliefs affect the lives of Muslims.

◎ Interpret some quotations from the Qur'an.

◎ Reflect on how to express your own ideas about ultimate questions and consider a Muslim's views.

Lesson 6: What does the Guru Granth Sahib mean to Sikhs?

◎ Consider what a guru is.

◎ Learn what the Guru Granth Sahib says about God.

◎ Interpret passages from the Guru Granth Sahib.

◎ Apply Sikh principles in daily life.

◎ Find out how Sikhs use the Guru Granth Sahib in worship.

1. How are Jewish scriptures used?

SKILLS

- **evaluating** some extracts from the Jewish Bible
- **matching** quotations from the Tenakh with pictures of aspects of Jewish life
- **explaining** why the Torah is important for Jews
- **learning and using** technical vocabulary correctly

ⓘ What is the Tenakh?

As we saw in Unit Three, the Jewish Bible is called the Tenakh. It comprises three sections:

1. **Torah**. This word means 'law'. For Jews, the Torah provides instructions on how to live, given by God himself.

2. **Nevi'im**. Nevi'im means 'prophets'. This section contains the writings of those people who believed that God had given them messages for the Jewish people.

3. **Ketuvim**. This means 'writings'. The Ketuvim are books of poetry, wise sayings and stories.

The word 'Tenakh' is made up of the initial letters of its three sections.

ⓘ What is the Torah about?

The most important part of the Tenakh is the Torah. It consists of five books, sometimes called the Books of Moses. For Jews, the Torah explains their relationship with God, and the conditions and laws God lays down for keeping that relationship. The laws cover every aspect of life, including how to worship, how to behave to

ACTIVITY ONE ....

Some of the Ketuvim contain wise sayings about life in general. Here are some examples.

'Better is open rebuke than hidden love. Wounds from a friend can be trusted, but an enemy multiplies kisses.'

(Proverbs 27:5–6)

'Before his downfall a man's heart is proud, but humility comes before honour.'

(Proverbs 18:12)

'Better what the eye sees than the roving of the appetite. This too is meaningless, a chasing after the wind.'

(Ecclesiastes 6:9)

'Do not withhold discipline from a child; if you punish him with the rod, he will not die. Punish him with the rod and save his soul from death.'

(Proverbs 23:13–14)

1. Explain what each of these sayings means.

2. Do you agree with them? Give reasons and examples to back up your answers.

others, how to conduct business and how to live at home. There are 613 of them, and they are called **mitzvot**. Ten of them are particularly famous, and are called the Ten Commandments. The Torah is so important that sometimes the whole of the Tenakh is called the Torah.

ACTIVITY TWO ....•••

Here are some examples of mitzvot from the Torah.

a) *'Observe the month of Abib [Spring] and celebrate the Passover of the LORD your God, because in the month of Abib he brought you out of Egypt by night.'*

(Deuteronomy 16:1)

b) *'Fix these words of mine in your hearts and minds; tie them as symbols on your hands and bind them on your foreheads.'*

(Deuteronomy 11:18)

c) *'These are the animals you may eat: the ox, the sheep, the goat, the deer … However … the pig is … unclean.'*

(Deuteronomy 14:4–8)

d) *'"Make tassels on the corners of your garments, with a blue cord on each tassel."'*

(Numbers 15:38)

e) *'Write them [the commandments] on the door-frames of your houses and on your gates.'*

(Deuteronomy 6:9)

f) *'"I give this land, from the river of Egypt to the great river, the Euphrates".'*

(Genesis 15:18)

Match them up with the pictures of various aspects of Jewish life, below.

ⓘ How is the Torah used?

▲ *A Sefer Torah and below the items with which the Torah is dressed.*

The copies of the Torah that are used in worship in the synagogue are handwritten on scrolls. They are called **Sefer Torah**. A person who writes a Torah scroll is called a **scribe**. It is written in the **Hebrew** language.

When the Sefer Torah is not in use, it is dressed. It is wrapped in a velvet cover, called a **mantle** (A), and a silver breastplate (B) is hung around the mantle. Silver crowns with bells (C) are placed on the tops of the rollers. A **yad** (D) (pointer for reading) is also hung from one of the rollers.

The scroll is then put into a cupboard, called the Aaron Hakodesh (**Ark**).

Jews believe that the Torah is the word of God, but they don't all agree what that means. Orthodox Jews believe that the commandments are God's law, given to them through Moses, to be interpreted and obeyed. Progressive Jews see the commandments as guidelines that should be adapted to suit the times. Nevertheless, the Torah is treated with great respect by all Jews.

When the scroll is to be read, it is taken out of the cupboard and carried around the synagogue. At special times, whoever is carrying it will dance. People try to touch it. It is then uncovered and held up high for all to see. When a person reads from it, the yad is used, to avoid touching the parchment. When a scroll becomes damaged with age, it may be repaired by a scribe. When it is beyond repair, it is put into permanent storage.

ACTIVITY THREE ••••••••••••

1. Why is the Torah important for Jews?
2. How do Jews show their respect for the Torah?

NOW TRY THIS ••••••••••

Write down ways in which the Sefer Torah is treated like a person. Why do you think this is so?

ACTIVITY FOUR ••••••••••••••

Write down sentences using the following words. Your sentences must not be definitions, but they should still make it clear what each word means. For example, 'David used a yad to help him follow the text when he read from the Torah' both uses the word 'yad', and explains what it means.

Ark   Sefer Torah   mantle   yad
Hebrew   mitzvot   scribe

2. What does the Bible teach Christians about God?

SKILLS

- **selecting information** from biblical quotations
- **interpreting** some passages from the Bible
- **judging** what is fair
- **interpreting and creating** your own parable

ⓘ What does the Christian Bible consist of?

The Christian Bible is a collection of 66 books. The first three quarters of it, 39 books, is called the Old Testament. It is the same as the Tenakh, the Jewish Bible, though the books are in a different order.

In addition, there are a further fourteen Jewish books, which are not in the Tenakh. They are called the **Apocrypha**, which means 'hidden' books.

Some Christians include them in the Bible, but others do not. There are two main reasons why the Jewish Bible is included in the Christian Bible:

1. Jesus was Jewish, and the first Christians were Jewish. The Tenakh was their scripture.

2. The Jewish Bible says that God was to send a great leader, like a king. He is called the Messiah. Christians believe that Jesus was the Messiah. The word 'Messiah' is Hebrew. Its Greek equivalent is 'Christos', so Christians are those people who believe that Jesus was the Messiah. This is why they call him Jesus Christ.

The second section of the Bible is called the New Testament. It contains information about the life and teachings of Jesus (the **Gospels**), the history and teachings of the first Christians, and one book of prophecy.

ACTIVITY ONE

This is what some of the prophets of the Old Testament had to say about what the Messiah would be like.

'He was despised and rejected by men, a man of sorrows, and familiar with suffering. Like one from whom men hide their faces he was despised, and we esteemed him not.' (Isaiah 53:3)

'"The days are coming … when I will raise up to David a righteous Branch, a King who will reign wisely and do what is just and right in the land."' (Jeremiah 23:5)

'By oppression and judgement he was taken away.' (Isaiah 53:8)

'He will not judge by what he sees with his eyes, or decide what he hears with his ears; but with righteousness he will judge the needy.' (Isaiah 11:3–4)

'The virgin will be with child and will give birth to a son.' (Isaiah 7:14)

'Then will the eyes of the blind be opened and the ears of the deaf by unstopped. Then will the lame leap like a deer, and the mute tongue shout for joy.' (Isaiah 35:5–6)

'"Bethlehem … out of you will come for me one who will be ruler over Israel".' (Micah 5:2)

'See, your king comes to you, righteous and having salvation.' (Zechariah 9:9)

Use these quotations to answer the following questions.

1. Where would the Messiah be born?
2. Who would the Messiah's mother be?
3. Into which family would the Messiah be born?
4. What would the Messiah be like?
5. What would the Messiah do for other people?
6. What would the Messiah's attitude to other people be like?
7. How would people treat the Messiah?
8. How would the Messiah die?

ACTIVITY TWO

1. Read the quotations from the gospels below. Use them, and your answers to the questions in Activity One, to explain why Christians believe that Jesus was the Messiah.

   'Jesus Christ the son of David, the son of Abraham.' (Matthew 1:1)

   'And they crucified him.' (Mark 15:24)

   'Jesus was born in Bethlehem in Judea.' (Matthew 2:1)

   'Again and again they struck him on the head with a staff and spat on him.' (Mark 15:19)

   'God sent the angel Gabriel to Nazareth, a town in Galilee, to a virgin … The virgin's name was Mary.' (Luke 1:26)

2. Why might some people not accept that Jesus was the Messiah?

ⓘ What is a parable?

The kingdom over which the Messiah would rule would be called the Kingdom of God. Jesus' ideas about the Kingdom of God were different from those of his fellow Jews. He taught about what it was like using stories that his listeners would understand. Stories that are told to illustrate a teaching are called **parables**. Some of them are quite difficult to understand.

A parable about the Kingdom of God

Early one morning a man went out to hire some workers for his vineyard. After he had agreed their pay, he sent them off to work. At about nine o'clock, the man saw some other people standing around. They agreed a rate of pay, and went off to work. At about three in the afternoon, and again at five he made the same arrangement with other workers.

That evening the vineyard owner called the workers in to pay them. When they arrived, the ones who had been hired at five in the afternoon were given a full day's pay. So were the ones hired at three, and those hired at midday.

The workers who had been hired first thought that they would be given even more than the others. But when they were given the same, they began complaining. The owner answered one of them,

'Friend, I didn't cheat you. I paid you exactly what we agreed on. Take your money and go! What business is it of yours if I want to pay others the same that I paid you? Don't I have the right to do what I want with my own money? Why should you be jealous, if I want to be generous?'

ACTIVITY THREE ············

1. Do you think that the owner of the vineyard was right to treat his workers in the way he did? Give reasons to support your answer.

2. How might the workers who complained have answered the vineyard owner's questions in the last paragraph of the story?

ACTIVITY FOUR ··

1. Here are some possible explanations of the meaning of the parable.

   a) God can be hard on people.

   b) Each person has a unique and personal relationship with God.

   c) People should be prepared to share.

   d) Life is unfair.

   e) Everyone is equal.

   f) The Kingdom of God is a place with rules that are completely different from the ones we are used to.

   g) The Kingdom of God is not a place. It is a frame of mind, an attitude to life.

   h) People shouldn't be concerned with wealth: there are far more important things in life.

   i) We can't understand how God works.

   j) Our idea of justice is wrong.

   Discuss each of these possibilities with a partner. Try to put them in a rank order, with the most likely meaning at the top, and the least likely at the bottom.

2. Jesus said that the parable means this: 'Everyone who is now first will be last, and everyone who is last will be first.' What do you think he meant?

NOW TRY THIS ·············

Write your own parable to illustrate *one* of the following:

- Don't judge people by their appearance.

- Things that aren't planned are likely to go wrong.

- Even the worst situations have some good in them.

KEY WORDS

Apocrypha   fourteen Jewish books not included in the Tenakh, but included in some versions of the Christian Bible

Gospels   four accounts of the life and teachings of Jesus in the Christian Bible

Parable   a story told to illustrate another meaning or moral point

3. How do the Buddhist scriptures guide people's lives?

SKILLS

- **thinking about** different ways of communicating
- **interpreting** a religious story
- **using symbols** to express ideas
- **evaluating** extracts from the Dhammapada

ⓘ The Buddha

Siddhartha Gautama was 35 years old when he became enlightened. He had learned how to overcome suffering and understand life at its deepest level. From this time onwards, he was known as the Buddha.

Siddhartha spent the next 45 years of his life, until his death, travelling around northern India, teaching others about the true nature of life and how to achieve perfect and permanent happiness.

My wisdom is as vast as the universe. I think I'll become a teacher!

ACTIVITY ONE ●●●●●●●●●●●●●●●●●●

People communicate their ideas and feelings to others in all sorts of ways – not just using words.

1. How could you let someone else know, without speaking, that:
   a) you are pleased to see them
   b) you are bored
   c) you are angry
   d) you hate them
   e) it's time to go?

2. List as many ways as you can that people use to communicate with each other without the use of words.

The Buddha taught a huge range of different people, all with different abilities to understand. So he had to use a variety of techniques to get his message across. After he died, the people who heard his teachings got together to agree on what he had taught. Eventually, these teachings were written down and form the Buddhist scriptures.

ⓘ What do the Buddhist scriptures consist of?

Legend has it that there are 80,000 teachings of the Buddha. That works out at about five lessons a day, 365 days a year for 45 years! The main collection is divided into three sections. Each section is called a 'pitaka', which means 'basket'. Together they are called the 'Tipitaka' (Three Baskets). They are:

1. **Sutta** Pitaka: The Buddha's teachings about life.

2. **Abhidhamma** Pitaka: Teachings about the teachings (i.e. explanations).

3. **Vinaya** Pitaka: Rules for Buddhist monks.

One of the most popular parts of the Sutta Pitaka is a collection of 547 stories called the **Jataka**. These are tales that illustrate truths about life. In Buddhist communities they are told to children in school and as bedtime stories. Here is an example.

The Dancing Peacock

Once upon a time, the birds chose the most beautiful of them all to be their king: a golden swan. The King's daughter was also beautiful and golden. When she was young, she was granted one wish. Her wish was that, when she grew up, she would be allowed to choose her husband, rather than have him chosen for her.

When she was older, the time came for the princess-swan to get married. The King gathered together all the male birds from every corner of the land. The princess looked them all over carefully before she stopped in front of a peacock. He had a slender, emerald-green neck and luxurious, flowing tail-feathers. 'This one,' the princess announced to her father, 'will be my husband.'

The other birds were naturally disappointed, but they congratulated the peacock, nevertheless, for being chosen as the most handsome of all the handsome birds. The peacock became swollen-headed with pride. He began to show off his colourful feathers in a fantastic, strutting dance. He fanned out his spectacular tail-feathers and puffed out his chest.

He stretched his neck upwards and pointed his head to the sky. In his conceit, he did not realise that everyone could see his bottom!

The younger birds giggled, but the King was embarrassed and angry. 'I cannot allow my daughter to marry someone so big-headed that he forgets all modesty,' he thought.

'Sir,' he said to the peacock, 'Your voice is sweet, your feathers are beautiful, your neck shines like an emerald and your tail is magnificent. But you have shown by your dancing that you have neither shame nor fear. I will not let my daughter marry a fool such as you!'

The princess was married to a royal nephew, and the silly, strutting peacock flew home, having lost a beautiful wife.

ACTIVITY TWO ....

What are the messages that this story illustrates? Suggest at least three.

ACTIVITY THREE ....

In small groups, devise a short story, and act it out using different ways of communicating. The rest of the class should try to work out what the story is.

Another popular part of the Sutta Pitaka is a collection of the Buddha's sayings, known as the **Dhammapada**. It consists of 423 verses which summarise the teachings of Buddhism. Here are some examples:

'Mind is the forerunner of all evil states. Our life is the creation of our mind. If one speaks or acts with an impure mind, suffering follows one as the wheel of the cart follows the ox that draws the cart.'

'Mind is the forerunner of all good states. Our life is the creation of our mind. If one speaks or acts with a pure mind, happiness follows one as his own shadows that never leaves.'

'Like a flower that is lovely and beautiful, but has no scent, even well-spoken words bear no fruit if one does not put them into practice.'

'The fool who knows that he is a fool is, for that very reason, a wise man; the fool who thinks that he is wise is called a fool indeed.'

'Just as a solid rock is not shaken by the wind, the wise are not moved by praise or blame.'

ACTIVITY FOUR ....

1. Put each of the sayings from the Dhammapada into your own words.

2. Evaluate them. In other words, say whether you agree or disagree with each of them. Give reasons for your opinion, and say why someone may have a point of view that is different from yours.

KEY WORDS

Abhidamma   Buddhist scripture explaining the Buddha's teachings in detail

Dhammapada   Buddhist scripture containing sayings of the Buddha

Jataka   stories about the Buddha's previous lives

Sutta   Buddhist scripture containing the Buddha's teaching

Vinaya   Buddhist scripture containing rules for monks and nuns

NOW TRY THIS ....

妙法蓮華経

This is the title of the Lotus Sutra, a popular Buddhist scripture, written in classical Chinese. It is pronounced, 'Myoho Renge Kyo'. Some Buddhists believe that writing or chanting it enables them to become enlightened. The lotus flower grows out of mud, and, for Buddhists, is a symbol that anyone can become enlightened.

Design a poster using the Chinese characters and an illustration of a lotus flower to express Buddhist ideas about enlightenment.

4. What are the Hindu scriptures about?

SKILLS

- **expressing** your own thoughts about harmful mental and verbal actions
- **interpreting** religious texts
- **identifying** significant events in the Ramayana
- **designing** a storyboard

You can't learn all there is to know about maths from just one book. There are different books for the different branches of maths, like geometry and trigonometry, and different books for different age groups and abilities.

In the same way, there is no single book that is special to Hindus. Different books give different insights into different aspects of life at different levels.

ⓘ What do the Hindu scriptures consist of?

There are two categories of books: **Shruti** and **Smriti**. The Shruti are the primary scriptures, revealed to sages in ancient times. The Smriti were written by wise men to explain the Shruti.

Shruti scriptures include the four Vedas (Rig, Yajur, Sama and Atharva). Each of them is divided into four parts: Samhita (hymns), Brahmana (teachings about ritual), Aranyaka (religious teachings), and Upanishads (explanations).

The Smriti consists of Ithasas (history), Puranas (mythology), Dharma Shastras (law codes, including the Laws of Manu), Agamas and Tantras (mystic literature), and Darshanas (Philosophy). The Ithasas include two epic poems: the **Ramayana** and the Mahabharata. The last part of the Mahabharata is called the Bhagavad Gita, the most famous of the Hindu scriptures.

ACTIVITY ONE ⋯⋯⋯⋯⋯⋯

Here is an extract from the **Laws of Manu**:

'Being jealous of other people's property, thinking in one's heart of what is not desirable, and believing in false teachings are three kinds of harmful mental action.'

'Speaking harshly to others, lying, slandering, and gossiping are four kinds of harmful verbal action.'

Can you think of two more harmful mental actions, and two more harmful verbal actions?

▲ *This picture shows an illustration in the* **Bhagavata Purana.** *The mythical creature underneath Brahma and Vishnu is Sesha Nag (Sesha the serpent).*

ⓘ What do the Upanishads say?

Most Hindus do not read all of the Vedas. Instead, they learn about Hindu philosophy from the Upanishads. This example explains the Hindu belief that the soul of each person is God: God is everything, and everything is God. It takes the form of a dialogue between a father and his son.

"'As bees, my son, make honey by collecting pollen from a number of different trees, and reduce the pollen to one form; and as the pollen is no longer separate, so it may say, 'I came from this tree or that one,' in the same manner, all creatures, when they have become merged in the True, do not know that they are merged in the true."

"Please, Sir, tell me more."

"Very well, my child," the father replied, "Place some salt in water, and come back to me in the morning."

The son did as he was told. The father said to him, "Bring me the salt you put in water last night." The son looked for it, but, of course, could not find it because it had dissolved.

The father said, "Taste it from the surface. How is it?" The son replied, "It is salty."

"Taste it from the bottom. How is it?" The son replied, "It is salty."

Then the father said, "In your own body you do not see the True, but it is there. It is the soul, and you are it."'

(Chandogya Upanishad, Prapathaka VI)

ACTIVITY TWO ••••••••••••••••

Try to explain in your own words what the **analogies** about bees and honey and salt in water mean. Try to think of your own analogy to express the same idea.

ⓘ What is the Ramayana?

The Ramayana is one of the two great Hindu epic poems that form the Ithasas (history books). It is much loved and children are brought up with it.

It is the story of Prince Rama. Rama's stepmother does not want him to become king, so he is sent away into the forest with his wife, Sita, and brother, Laksmana.

There they meet a female demon, who falls in love with Rama. Rama refuses her, and Laksmana wounds her; she runs away to her brother, Ravana, the ruler of the island of Lanka. When Ravana hears how beautiful Sita is, he goes into the forest, kidnaps her, and takes her back to Lanka.

▶ **The story of Rama and Sita is still very popular in Hindu culture. This painting shows the moment when Rama and Laksmana ask Hanuman to help them find Sita.**

Rama and Laksmana ask the monkey king, Hanuman, to help them find Sita. Hanuman, who is able to change his size, steps over the sea to Lanka. He finds Sita but is caught by Ravana, who sets his tail on fire. Still, Hanuman escapes with Sita.

Rama, Laksmana, Hanuman and an army of monkeys declare war on Lanka. The monkeys form a chain to act as a bridge to the island. After a long battle, Rama kills Ravana. Rama, not convinced that Sita has been faithful to him on Lanka, asks that she prove herself to him by sitting in fire. She does, and comes out unharmed.

Still, rumours spread that Sita has been disloyal, so she is banished to a religious community. There she gives birth to twin sons. Eventually, the family is reunited. Sita decides to prove her loyalty by asking the earth to swallow her up. Rama then decides to end his own life by jumping into a river.

▲ *This illustration from an Islamic book shows the siege of Lanka, and the fighting between the demons and the monkeys. What reasons could there be for an Islamic book to depict a Hindu epic?*

ACTIVITY THREE ··············

Imagine you are making a cartoon or video game based on the Ramayana.

1. Decide which are the six most important scenes in the story.
2. Explain why you think these are the most important scenes.
3. Draw them up as a storyboard.

NOW TRY THIS ·············

The Ramayana is very popular because it is about important values, like love, honesty, determination, courage, freedom and loyalty. The story is celebrated in different Hindu festivals.

a) What other values does the story depict?

b) Draw a symbol for each of the values.

KEY WORDS

Analogy   comparing a complicated idea with something more simple and familiar, to help explain it

Laws of Manu   collection of twelve Hindu books containing instructions in law and ethics

Ramayana   the story of Rama and Sita

Shruti   'what is heard'; Hindu scriptures believed to have come from God

Smriti   'what is remembered'; Hindu scriptures written to explain the Shruti

5. What does the Qur'an tell us about Islamic beliefs?

SKILLS

- **selecting** information from religious texts
- **interpreting** quotations from the Qur'an
- **inferring** how belief might affect behaviour
- **expressing** your own views on ultimate questions

ⓘ What is the Qur'an?

Muslims believe that the Qur'an was revealed to Muhammad by Allah (God). For Muslims, therefore, its words are the words of God. Because Muhammad was an Arab, the Qur'an was revealed in Arabic. The Prophet would recite what he had heard to his secretary, who would then read it back. Shortly after Muhammad's death in 632 CE, the individual revelations were collected together to form one book. It is believed that the Qur'an today is exactly the same as that which was revealed to Muhammad at the beginning of the seventh century.

The Qur'an reveals seven basic beliefs that are central to Islam.

1. Tawhid – The oneness of God

'He is Allah, the One. Allah is eternal and absolute. None is born of Him, nor is He born. And there is none like him.' (Surah (Chapter) 112)

2. Mala'ikah – Angels

'Angels are appointed over you to protect you; they are kind and honourable, and write down your deeds. They know and understand all you do.'

(Surah 82:10–12)

We believe in angels. They have been created by God from light, and so cannot be seen, unless they take on human form. Unlike humans, they do have free will, and so cannot disobey God. The Qur'an teaches that angels watch over us and write down everything that we say and do.

3. Kutubullah – Books of God

'Those who say, "God does not send down revelations to humans," are wrong. Tell them, "So who sent down the book that Moses brought – a light and guidance to the human race?" But you have made it into separate books and left out a lot of it … But this book which We have sent down brings blessings.'

(Surah 6:91–92)

God has given us his guidance in the past in the form of various books: the Torah, the Psalms of David, the Gospel of Jesus, and, of course, the Qur'an. But the first three of these have become corrupted, and only the Qur'an contains the pure words of Allah.

Tawhid means the oneness of God. We Muslims believe that nothing could exist or happen without him: he is all-knowing, all-wise and all-powerful. Believing in Allah and submitting to his will makes us humble and modest as people. Since Allah takes care of all of our needs, we are contented. We are able to face life with courage, because belief in Allah takes away our fear of death. This makes us confident and gives us dignity.

4. Rusulullah – Messengers of God

'God sent messengers with both good news and with warnings.' (Surah 2:213)

God communicates with us through specially chosen human beings called prophets. This is how he gives us his guidance so that we can do as he wishes and lead good lives. The Qur'an tells us about 25 of the prophets, including Abraham, Moses and Jesus. The last and the greatest of the prophets was Muhammad (peace be upon him).

5. Al-Qadr – Predestination

'Nobody knows what they will earn tomorrow, nor does anyone know in what land they are to die. Only Allah has full knowledge and is acquainted with all things.' (Surah 31:34)

Allah created the universe and is in absolute control of everything that happens. Nothing happens unless he wishes it to. We don't know what will happen to us, but Allah does. This is called predestination – Al-Qadr.

6. Yawmuddin – Day of Judgement

'We shall set up scales of justice for the day of judgement so that nobody will be treated unfairly.' (Surah 21:47)

We believe that angels record everything we do. One day, the world will end and there will be a day of judgement – Yawmuddin. Angels will show us the record of our lives, and God will judge us. Good people will be rewarded, but evil-doers will be punished.

7. Akhirah – Life after death

'We have made all humans to die, but We will then change you and create you again in forms that you do not know of.' (Surah 56:60–61)

We believe that death does not mean the end of us. Life on earth is a preparation for Akhirah – eternal life. After the day of judgement, we will go either to Paradise, or to Hell.

ACTIVITY ONE ....

1. What do Muslims believe about God?

2. Christians believe that Jesus was the Son of God; Muslims do not. Why not?

3. In what ways is this life a preparation for life after death, according to Islamic belief?

ACTIVITY TWO ....

Give one example of how each of the seven basic Islamic beliefs would affect the way a Muslim would conduct his or her life.

ACTIVITY THREE ....

'If God punished people according to what they deserved, he would not leave on earth a single living thing.'

(Surah 16:61)

1. What does this mean?

2. What does it say about what God is like?

3. Do you believe that there is life after death? Give reasons.

4. Do you have to be religious to believe in life after death? Say why you do, or do not.

ACTIVITY FOUR ....

1. If there is a God who knows and controls everything, how could he allow suffering?

2. What answer would a Muslim give?

3. Discuss these questions with a partner.

NOW TRY THIS ....

How might living in a country in which most people are Muslims be different from living in Britain?

6. What does the Guru Granth Sahib mean to Sikhs?

SKILLS

- **identifying** the characteristics of a guru
- **interpreting** text from the Guru Granth Sahib
- **applying** Sikh teachings to daily life
- **linking** information from previous lessons to Sikhism

ⓘ What is a guru?

The leader of the Sikh community is called a guru. A guru has the following functions:

- teacher
- spiritual leader
- community leader
- religious authority.

ACTIVITY ONE

1. The word *guru* comes from the same root as the word grave (serious), which comes from the Latin word *gravis*. Find out what *gravis* means, and explain what it has to do with the role of the guru.
2. What sort of qualities should a guru have?

ⓘ What does the Guru Granth Sahib consist of?

For 200 years, until the beginning of the eighteenth century, the guru was a human being. In 1699, the tenth human guru, Guru Gobind Singh, appointed the eleventh: it was to be a book of religious writings. The original book, called the **Adi Granth**, had been compiled by the fifth guru. It consisted of the writings of the first five gurus, and some Hindu and Muslim writings. Guru Gobind Singh added writings of the ninth guru, and his own, to form the Guru Granth Sahib.

For Sikhs, the Guru Granth Sahib contains God's guidance on the spiritual and moral life; in other words, how to live as a human being in relation to God and in relation to other people. There are teachings on a number of subjects, which you can read about on the next page.

▼ *The Guru Granth Sahib is written in the Punjabi language in a script called Gurmukhi.*

These are some of the things the Guru Granth Sahib says about God.

'God neither dies nor is there any need to grieve for Him.'

(Asa M.1)

'God alone gives and His givings know no bounds.'

(Asa M.1)

'You alone know, see and do, O Lord.'

(Asa M.4.f:2)

'O You, the knower of our inmost desires!'

(Gauri Poorbi M.5.4:5)

'He who gave us life and soul, gives us also peace when He comes into us.'

(Sri Rag M.1)

'It is by realising God in our inner selves that He blesses us with His grace and washes our dirt off.'

(Sri Rag M.1.3:12)

'True He is and truth it is that He loves.'

(Sri Rag M.1)

'Infinite love is the speech of God.'

(Jap 1.4)

'The Lord is my friend. He alone is my support in the end.'

(Sri Rag M.3)

'He is your creator, your transcendent God.'

(Sri Rag M.1)

Here are some more quotations from the Guru Granth Sahib.

'Nobody can take responsibility for a thief. How can any action of a thief be good?'

(Guru I, Dhanasri Rag)

'Whosoever is kind to others, the Lord receives him with kindness.'

(Guru V, Gauri Rag)

'In this universe, I behold, what can a man get without exertion?'

(Guru I, Japji)

'Whoever thinks high of themselves and low of others, I saw them going to hell.'

(Kabiriji, Maru Rag)

'If you seek God, do not break the heart of another.'

(Farid, Shlokas)

'Finish your task with your own effort.'

(Guru I, Asa Rag)

'Only fools and idiots try to suppress others.'

(Guru I, Basant Rag)

'Think everyone your dear friend.'

(Guru V, Asa Rag)

'Ignorance hinders progress.'

(Kabirji, Asa Rag)

ACTIVITY TWO

Read the quotations from the Guru Granth Sahib above and then use at least four adjectives to describe what Sikhs believe God to be like.

ACTIVITY THREE

Write a list of ten school rules based on the principles above from the Guru Granth Sahib.

ⓘ How do Sikhs show respect for the Guru Granth Sahib?

As the eleventh guru, the Guru Granth Sahib is treated with the same respect that an important human being would be. It is the focal point of Sikh worship, placed at the front of the Prayer Hall in a gurdwara (Sikh temple) and raised above the level of the worshippers on a throne, called a **takht**, under a canopy called a **chanani**. The Granth is never left unattended, and when it is being read a **chauri**, a sort of fan, is waved over it to protect it.

Worshippers remove their shoes and cover their heads before entering a room where the Guru Granth Sahib is present. They bow and make offerings to it. They sit on the floor, and never turn their backs or feet towards it.

When it is not being used, the Guru Granth Sahib is carried in a procession, above the heads of the people, to its own room. Here it is wrapped up carefully, laid on a bed and covered over.

▲ *The Guru Granth Sahib being fanned with a chauri by a granthi during a reading.*

ACTIVITY FOUR ⋅⋅⋅⋅⋅⋅⋅⋅⋅⋅⋅⋅⋅⋅

1. Choose three phrases from the information above that show why the Guru Granth Sahib is sometimes called the Living Guru.

2. How does the way the Guru Granth Sahib is treated reflect this title?

KEY WORDS

Adi Granth   the first Sikh holy book, compiled by the fifth guru

Chanani   canopy under which the Guru Granth Sahib rests when being read

Chauri   whisk or fan waved over the Guru Granth Sahib to protect it

Takht   padded throne on which the Guru Granth Sahib rests when being read

NOW TRY THIS ⋅⋅⋅⋅⋅⋅⋅⋅⋅⋅⋅⋅⋅

'Let kindness be your mosque,
Faith be your prayer-mat,
Honest earnings be your Qur'an, …
And good conduct be your fast.'

(Guru I, Majh Rag)

'Mechanical repetition of mantras, …
Lectures on the Shrutis and the Smritis,
The practice of Yoga, the religious rites and rituals,
And observance of fasts and vows and other deeds,
With all these, the dirt of ego will not depart.'

(Guru V, Gauri Rag)

'What are all these rituals worth, if the heart is not sincere?'

(Namdevji, Asa Rag)

a) Which two religions are being referred to in these quotations from the Guru Granth Sahib? Back up your answer with evidence.

b) What is the Sikh view of the ritual aspect of religion?

SUMMARY OF UNIT 4

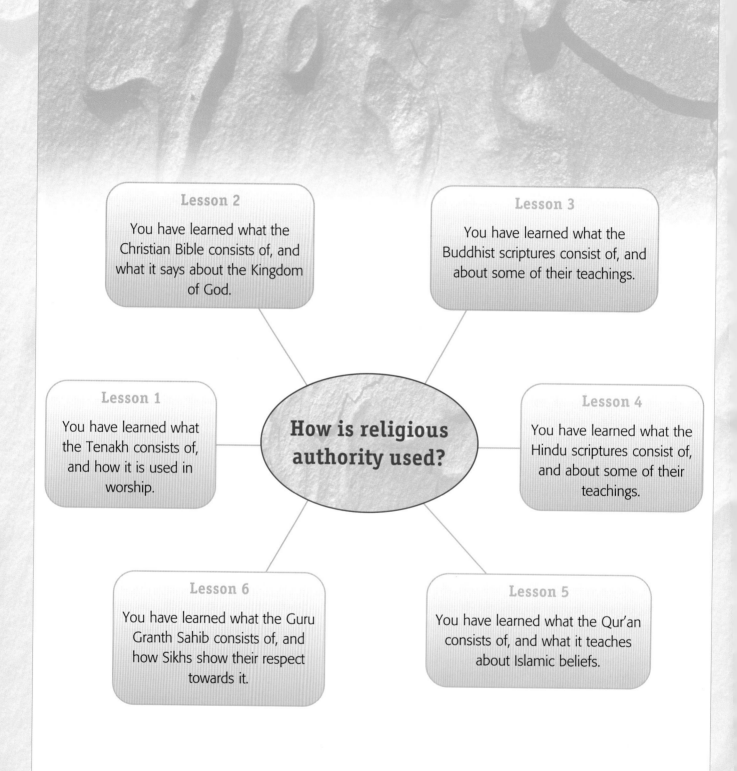

Lesson 2

You have learned what the Christian Bible consists of, and what it says about the Kingdom of God.

Lesson 3

You have learned what the Buddhist scriptures consist of, and about some of their teachings.

Lesson 1

You have learned what the Tenakh consists of, and how it is used in worship.

How is religious authority used?

Lesson 4

You have learned what the Hindu scriptures consist of, and about some of their teachings.

Lesson 6

You have learned what the Guru Granth Sahib consists of, and how Sikhs show their respect towards it.

Lesson 5

You have learned what the Qur'an consists of, and what it teaches about Islamic beliefs.

UNIT 5: WHAT DOES RELIGION SAY ABOUT BEING HUMAN?

Lesson 1: What do Christians, Jews and Muslims say it means to be human?

◎ Decide what makes human beings different from animals.

◎ Find out what Christian, Jewish and Islamic scriptures teach about what a human is.

◎ Find out what Christian, Jewish and Islamic scriptures teach about the role of human beings in the world.

◎ Read about and form your own opinion on the responsibility human beings have for animals and their natural environment.

Lesson 2: What do Hindus, Sikhs and Buddhists say it means to be human?

◎ Discover Hindu and Sikh ideas about the soul.

◎ Learn about the Buddhist view that all beings are connected.

◎ Consider what a human being is.

◎ Form your own opinion on whether or not human beings should be vegetarian.

Lesson 3: Are we in control of what we do?

◎ Consider whether human beings have free will.

◎ Find out what free will means to Christians and Muslims.

◎ Think about how we are responsible for what happens to us.

◎ Decide for yourself if we are in control of what we do.

Lesson 4: Are we in control of what happens to us?

◎ Identify the similarities and differences between what Hindus and Buddhists believe about karma.

◎ Find out about Hindu and Buddhist beliefs regarding life after death.

◎ Form your own opinion about karma and if you believe in it.

◎ Decide how believing in karma might affect a person's life and the way they choose to live it.

Lesson 5: What does Christianity teach about the world?

◎ Read about Christian views on the nature of good and evil.

◎ Think about the world, and how it is both good and bad.

◎ Consider the nature of evil, and how we know about right and wrong.

◎ Learn about Christian views on how evil is created.

Lesson 6: What do Buddhism and Hinduism teach about the world?

◎ Review the Hindu and Buddhist idea of samsara.

◎ Read about Hindu gods and the creation of the world according to Hindus.

◎ Learn about the differences between Hindu and Buddhist ideas regarding samsara.

◎ Evaluate the idea of samsara.

1. What do Christians, Jews and Muslims say it means to be human?

SKILLS

- **expressing** your opinions
- **listening** to the views of others
- **linking** religious teachings to the English language
- **thinking about** human responsibility for other animals

ACTIVITY ONE

Discuss your views about the following questions in small groups.

1. Do animals have a moral sense, i.e. a sense of right and wrong?
2. Do animals have life after death?
3. Do animals have emotions, like love or jealousy?
4. Are animals aware that they exist?
5. Do animals have rights?

From a scientific point of view, human beings are members of the animal kingdom. However, in many ways we are different from other animals.

▲ *Spot the difference.*

ACTIVITY TWO ••

Read the quotations below and then answer the questions that follow.

'We created Man [human beings] from the essence of clay, we made bones out of that lump and clothed the bones with flesh; then we developed out of it another creature.'

(Surah 23:12–14)

'The Lord said to the angels, "I am about to create Man from moulding clay into shape. When I have formed him and breathed my spirit into him, fall down in submission to him."'

(Surah 15:28–29)

'The LORD God formed the man from the dust of the ground and breathed into his nostrils the breath of life, and the man became a living being.'

(Genesis 2:7)

1. What do you think the first passage means when it says, 'we developed out of it another creature'?

2. According to these quotations, what are human beings?

▲ *'So the man gave names to all the livestock, the birds of the air and all the beasts of the field.' (Genesis 2:20). This painting is called* Paradiso Terrestre, *by Jacopo Bassano, showing God, Adam and the animals.*

ⓘ Religious quotations

'Then God said, "Let us make man in our image, in our likeness, and let them rule over the fish of the sea and the birds of the air, over the livestock, over all the earth, and over all the creatures that move along the ground." So God created man … male and female he created them. God blessed them and said to them, "Be fruitful and increase in number; fill the earth and subdue it. Rule over the fish of the sea and the birds of the air and over every living creature that moves on the ground."'

(Genesis 1:26–28)

'And the cattle he has created for you: from them you get warmth and numerous benefits, and you eat their meat … And he has created horses, mules and donkeys for you.'

(Surah 16:5–8)

ACTIVITY THREE

Read the quotations. Do you believe that human beings have control over other animals? Is it right that we should?

NOW TRY THIS

'Hereby is refuted the error of those who said it is sinful for a man to kill brute animals; for by the divine providence they are intended for man's use according to the order of nature. Hence it is not wrong for man to make use of them, either by killing or in any other way whatever.'

(Thomas Aquinas, a Christian theologian in the thirteenth century, *Summa Contra Gentiles 3:2*)

a) Do you think Aquinas has fairly presented the biblical view of the relationship between people and animals?

b) Do you agree with Aquinas? Give reasons to support your point of view.

ACTIVITY FOUR

1. What should the human attitude to animals be, according to the following quotations?

'You made him [man] a little lower than the heavenly beings and crowned him with glory and honour. You made him ruler over the works of your hands; you put everything under his feet; all flocks and herds, and the beasts of the field, the birds of the air, and the fish of the sea, all that swim the paths of the seas.'

(Psalm 8:5–8)

'The earth is the LORD'S, and everything in it, the world and all who live in it.'

(Psalm 24:1)

'To God belongs the authority over the heavens and the earth.'

(Surah 24:42)

2. Some chickens reared for human consumption are kept in the following conditions:

- less than 600cm^2 space per bird (about the size of a computer screen)
- never cleaned out: birds stand in their own droppings
- no windows; artificial light 23 hours a day to encourage them to eat
- they grow so large so fast, their bones break under the weight.

(Source: Viva – Vegetarians International Voice for Animals)

Why do humans treat animals in this way? Do you believe that animals should be treated with the same respect as humans?

2. What do Hindus, Sikhs and Buddhists say it means to be human?

SKILLS

- **interpreting** religious texts
- **describing** a person in non-physical terms
- **explaining** the Buddhist idea of anatta, using your own example
- **inferring** how Hindu and Buddhist beliefs might influence behaviour

KEY WORDS

Anatta   the idea that a fixed, permanent identity is an illusion (Buddhism)

Atman   the soul (Hinduism)

Moksha   freedom from the cycle of birth and death (Hinduism)

ⓘ What do Hindus believe about being human?

1. Hindus believe that everything that lives has a soul (**atman**). The atman forms a person's identity and personality. It lives forever, and does not change.

2. The soul lives forever, and is reborn into a series of temporary bodies.

3. Each individual's soul is part of God (Brahman).

4. Because the soul is God, people should not cause harm to each other.

5. The ultimate aim of Hinduism is for the soul to escape from being reborn, and to be reunited with God. This is called **moksha**.

ACTIVITY ONE

Match up the following quotations a–e from the Hindu scriptures with each of the paragraphs in the Information section above 1–5.

a) *'I shall tell you of the soul. The soul is God, who is immortal and infinite, who has no beginning and will have no end.'*

(Bhagavad Gita 13:12)

b) *'The soul is not born, but always exists. It is the consciousness of life, and dwells in every heart.'*

(Brihadaranyaka Upanishad 4:4.22)

c) *'If you see the soul in every living being, you see truly. If you see immortality in the heart of every mortal being, you see truly. If you see God within every man and woman, then you can never do harm to any man or woman.'*

(Bhagavad Gita 13:28)

d) *'If you fail to see God in the present life, then after death you must take on another body; if you see God, then you will break free from the cycle of birth and death.'*

(Katha Upanishad 6:13)

e) *'A goldsmith takes an old ornament and fashions it into a new and more beautiful one. In the same way the soul, as it leaves one body, looks for a new body which is more beautiful.'*

(Brihadaranyaka Upanishad 4:4.3)

ⓘ What do Sikhs believe about being human?

Sikhism follows Hindu teachings about the nature of a human being. These quotations are from the Guru Granth Sahib.

'The soul neither dies, nor can it be destroyed.'

(Guru V, Gond Rag)

'The body that you anoint with scented oils will be reduced to ashes one day.'

(Kabirji, Sri Rag)

'I took the form of so many plants and trees, and so many animals … Many times I entered the families of snakes and flying birds.'

(Guru I, Rag Gauree)

ACTIVITY TWO

The quotations from the Guru Granth Sahib opposite suggest that the body is the temporary home of the soul. The body is the part of a human being that can be discovered through the senses – seeing, touching, smelling, hearing and tasting. The soul is the part of a human being that cannot be sensed.

Divide into groups of six. Individually, write a description of someone else in the group *without mentioning anything that can be sensed*. Then read your description to the group, and see if they can guess whom it is about.

ⓘ What do Buddhists believe about being human?

Siddhartha Gautama, the Buddha, was born into a Hindu tradition. He understood the Hindu idea of a human as being a soul (atman) within a body. But he disagreed with it. He said that there was no such thing as a soul (**anatta**), and therefore no such thing as an individual. Buddhism says that individuality is an illusion. There is no you. Life is one thing that is shared by all living things. The body is just a collection of flesh and bones, thoughts and feelings.

One of the Buddhist scriptures is called The Questions of King Milinda. It takes the form of a series of discussions between Milinda, the king of India, and the Buddhist monk, Nagasena. Here they are talking about the existence of a fixed, permanent self, or soul.

Milinda: What is your name, monk?

Nagasena: I am known as Nagasena; but this is just a convenient label, because I have no fixed or permanent identity.

Milinda: If it is the case that people do not have fixed, permanent identities, then there is no one to provide you with the things you need to live. If someone were to kill you, there would be no murder, because there would be no 'you' to be killed. This is rubbish!

Nagasena: Think of it like this, Sir. How did you travel here today?

Milinda: In a chariot.

Nagasena: What is a chariot? Is it the axle, or the wheels, or the chassis, or the reins? Is it all of these together? Or is it something completely separate?

Milinda: Well, it's none of those.

Nagasena: So, there is no such thing as a chariot. It has no fixed identity. In the same way, what you see before you is not 'me', but just a collection of arms, legs, torso, head, thoughts and feelings.

What is a chariot?

ACTIVITY THREE ················

In the extract from the Questions of King Milinda, Nagasena compares a human being to a chariot. Can you think of a more modern object to compare a human to? How would the discussion go then?

Even though Buddhists disagree with Hindus and Sikhs about the existence of the soul, they all agree about the responsibility that humans have for their fellow human beings and the natural environment.

'He [God] is the eternal reality … and the ground of existence. Those who see him in every creature merge in him and are released from the wheel of birth and death.'

(*Shvetashvatara Upanishad* (Hinduism))

'The one who protects himself also protects other selves. You should thus protect yourself. Such a person will never receive harm and is a wise person.'

(*Anguttaranikaya* (Buddhism))

ACTIVITY FOUR ················

1. Why do you think most Hindus and Buddhists are vegetarian?
2. Why do you think some are not?

NOW TRY THIS ·············

'I do not see any reason why animals should be slaughtered to serve as human diet; there are so many substitutes. After all, man can live without meat.'

(Dali Lama, *The Vegetarian Way*)

The Dalai Lama is a senior Buddhist. Do you agree with what he says in this quotation? Why might someone disagree with you?

3. Are we in control of what we do?

SKILLS

- **thinking about** whether you are responsible for what happens to you
- **explaining** how you make decisions
- **discussing** whether or not human beings have free will

Why does it always happen to me?

ACTIVITY ONE

1. Imagine the following things happening to you. Are you responsible for them? Discuss them with a partner.

   - winning the lottery

   - being in detention for not doing homework

   - being mugged

   - entering but not winning the lottery

   - catching a cold

   - having a nightmare

   - being born with a disability

   - being bullied

   - failing an exam

   - passing an exam.

2. Do you believe in luck? Are some people lucky, or unlucky? Why do good things seem to happen to some people, but bad things to others?

Do we have control over our lives?

Christian

We believe that God created the world and human beings. He is in control of the world, but human beings have free will. This means that we are free to choose whether or not to believe in him. We are also free to choose what we say and do.

Muslim

We believe that God created the world and human beings. He is in control of the world, and of us. We have free will: we are able to choose whether to believe in God or not, and to choose what we say and do. However, God knows in advance what we will say and do – our lives are predestined.

ACTIVITY TWO ·················

Having free will means being able to make choices. How do you make the following choices:

a) which school to go to

b) which clothes to wear

c) who your friends are

d) whether or not you like pizza

e) whether or not to believe in God?

ACTIVITY THREE ••••••••••••••••••••••••••••••••••••••

Scientists are now beginning to discover that some of our characteristics and patterns of behaviour are **genetic**: we are programmed in some way before we are born.

a) Do you believe that the course of your life has been set in advance, or do you think you have control over it? Are there any parts you do not have control over? Give reasons for your answers.

b) If human beings were not in control of their lives, would a criminal be responsible for his or her actions?

▶ *An autoradiogram is a photographic record of a DNA sequence or a 'genetic fingerprint'.*

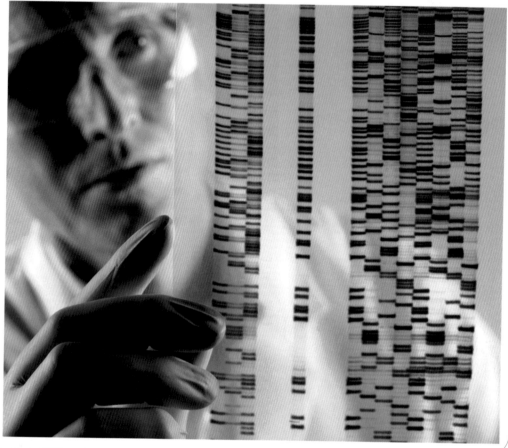

ACTIVITY FOUR ••••••••••••

If human beings have free will, does this mean that we are responsible for everything that we do? Are we also responsible for everything that happens to us?

Discuss this question in pairs, remembering to give reasons to support your opinions. Then write a summary of your discussion.

NOW TRY THIS ••••••••••••

The Prophet Muhammad was once asked why, if the course of a person's life has been set in advance, people should bother doing good deeds. The Prophet replied, 'Do you know what has been decided for you?'

a) What did Muhammad mean by his answer?

b) What answer would you have given?

KEY WORD

Genetic to do with the characteristics that are passed from parents to children during reproduction

4. Are we in control of what happens to us?

SKILLS

- **working out** how the past and future may be connected
- **explaining** what karma means
- **comparing** Hindu and Buddhist ideas about karma
- **expressing your opinion** about the idea of karma
- **inferring** how belief in karma might affect a person's life

ACTIVITY ONE

Read the story in the boxes. Write the next few episodes in Jay's life by drawing at least six more boxes and writing one sentence in each.

Jay receives a poor education.

Jay leaves school with no qualifications.

JOB CENTRE

Jay can't get a job.

Jay is born into a poor family.

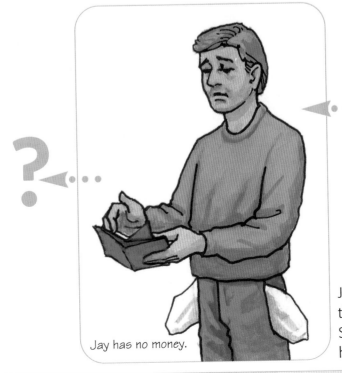

Jay has no money.

Jay blames his home background and bad luck for the things that have happened to him. Hindus, Buddhists and Sikhs do not believe this. They believe that everything happens for a reason. This idea is called **karma**.

ⓘ What is karma?

Hindus, Buddhists and Sikhs believe that events in a person's life are all connected. Events are caused by other events that happened in the past. It is you that make the causes, and it is you that receive the effects. This is called karma. The word 'karma' means 'action'. It means that nothing happens by chance. Your actions in the world are the cause of everything that happens to you, and so you are responsible for everything that happens to you.

Hinduism

Hindus believe in **reincarnation**. If a person has led a good life, their soul will be reborn in a new body in good circumstances. But a lifetime of bad deeds will result in a less favourable reincarnation. God has created the law of karma, just as he created the law of gravity. Like gravity, karma works on its own. So it is not right to say that God rewards or punishes people. People have free will, and so create their own karma.

Buddhism

Buddhists also believe in karma. They believe that you make your own future by how you choose to act now. Like Hindus, they believe that people are reborn in future lifetimes, but they do not separate these lifetimes. They see life and death as like being awake and being asleep: one continuous existence. So whatever happens to you, whether in this lifetime or another one, including natural events like illness, it is the result of karma. You are responsible for it.

▼ *Religious actions can produce good karma. Here a Buddhist applies gold paint to a statue of the Buddha.*

ACTIVITY TWO ......

Write a brief description of what *either* Hindus *or* Buddhists believe about karma. Then outline the similarities and differences between this and the other belief.

ACTIVITY THREE ...

Do you believe in karma? Give reasons and examples to support your answer.

ACTIVITY FOUR ....

How might believing in karma affect the way a person lives his or her life?

Hindus believe in reincarnation. This statue is of Lord Narayana reincarnated as Haragriva, the pure white Horse-god.

NOW TRY THIS ....

The word reincarnation can be broken down into three parts: *re-in-carnation*. The *-carnation* bit comes from the Latin word *carnis*.

a) Find out what *carnis* means. Then write down what *reincarnation* literally means.

b) Buddhists do not use the word *reincarnation*, but prefer to talk about *rebirth*. Why do you think this is?

KEY WORDS

Karma (action) the idea that your actions affect what will happen to you in the future

Reincarnation   the belief that the soul is reborn in another body

5. What does Christianity teach about the world?

SKILLS

- **presenting** your thoughts in the form of a leaflet
- **expressing** your ideas about how human beings know about right and wrong
- **comparing** moral situations
- **interpreting** religious texts

ⓘ The world is good

According to the story in the Old Testament, it took God six days to create the world. At the end of each day, the narrative says, God looked at what he had made, and 'it was good'. On the sixth day, he created human beings. At the end of that day, his creation is described as 'very good'.

ACTIVITY ONE ••••••••••••••••••

One of the points that the story of creation makes is that the world is basically good; that it is the best of all possible worlds.

Imagine you are an estate agent, and you have been instructed to sell planet earth. Your task is to produce a leaflet containing details about the world that emphasise its good points. You should also point out the things that are wrong, and make suggestions about how to improve them.

So Christians believe that God created the world as a place of goodness, and he created human beings to be good. Yet we know that human beings are not all good. How do Christians explain this? The following story from the Bible answers this question.

'God put the man that he had made into a garden in a place called Eden. He told him, "You may eat fruit from any tree, except the one in the middle of the garden: that one gives you the power to know the difference between right and wrong. If you do, you will die."

God then made a woman to be a suitable partner for the man. Although they were both naked, they were not embarrassed or ashamed.

The snake was the most cunning of the animals. One day he said to the woman, "Did God tell you not to eat the fruit from the tree in the middle of the garden?"

The woman answered, "Yes. He said that if we do, we will die."

"No, you won't," the snake replied. "What will happen is that you will know the difference between right and wrong just as God does."

The woman wanted to have the wisdom that God has, and she ate some of the fruit. She gave some to the man, and he ate it, too. Immediately, they saw what they had done, and they realised that they were naked. They sewed fig leaves together to cover themselves.

Later that day, they heard God walking in the garden. They were frightened and hid behind some trees.'

(Adapted from *Genesis* 2:7–3:8)

'"The woman you put here with me – she gave me some fruit from the tree, and I ate it."' (Genesis 3:12).
Adam and Eve by Jacopo Tintoretto, depicting Eve offering Adam the apple.

ACTIVITY TWO

This story explains that, although God created the world to be good, human beings introduced evil by choosing to disobey him. When human beings disobey God, they do so deliberately. They *know* what they are doing.

a) Do people always know when they are doing wrong?

b) If someone is not aware that what they are doing is wrong, is it still wrong?

c) Are people born good, and learn about right and wrong as they grow older, or are they born with the knowledge of right and wrong?

ACTIVITY THREE ●●●

1. Discuss the following scenarios with a partner. Put each of them on a scale of 0–10, where 10 is the most evil, and 0 the least. Give reasons for your decisions.

   a) A man kills another man who has attacked him with a knife.

   b) A youth mugs an old woman and steals £50.

   c) A car hits a child who has run out from behind a parked van. The driver had not been drinking and was driving within the speed limit.

   d) A toddler in a shop with his mother takes a bag of sweets. His mother sees but does nothing.

   e) A man shoots and kills a cashier while robbing a bank.

   f) A poor pensioner steals a tin of cat food from a supermarket.

   g) A toddler in a shop with his mother takes a bag of sweets. His mother does not see.

   h) A woman kills another woman who has had an affair with her husband.

   i) A cat takes a piece of chicken from a plate in the kitchen.

   j) Humans kill cattle for food.

   k) Humans kill tigers for their skins.

2. What makes one deed more or less evil than another?

ACTIVITY FOUR ●●●●●●●●●●●●●●

'"What comes out of a man is what makes him 'unclean'. For from within, out of men's hearts, come evil thoughts, sexual immorality [wickedness], theft, murder, adultery, greed, malice, deceit, lewdness, envy, slander, arrogance and folly."'

(Jesus in *Mark 7:20–22*)

What did Jesus mean by this?

NOW TRY THIS ●●●●●●●●●●●●

In the Genesis story of the Temptation, God punishes the snake, the man and the woman.

a) What punishments would you have given them in the circumstances?

b) Read *Genesis 3:9–19* in the Bible. Do you think that the punishments were fair? Why, or why not?

6. What do Buddhism and Hinduism teach about the world?

> ## SKILLS
> - **evaluating** the Buddhist idea of samsara
> - **interpreting** symbols in representations of Hindu gods
> - **representing** the Hindu idea of samsara in a diagram
> - **comparing** the Hindu and Buddhist ideas of samsara

We have seen that Hindus believe in reincarnation. When the body dies, it is burned to ashes and destroyed. But they believe that the soul (atman) lives on by moving to another body in another lifetime. This process is called **samsara**. The soul may be born into various life forms, like something non-animal (such as a rock or a tuft of grass), an animal, a human, or even a god.

Buddhists also believe in the ideas of rebirth and samsara, but their ideas differ.

ⓘ How do Buddhists think of samsara?

Buddhists use the idea of samsara in thinking about what the world is like, but they picture it differently from Hindus.

For Buddhists, life in our world is unsatisfactory: it doesn't satisfy us. Things go wrong, and we end up frustrated and unhappy. Buddhists call this **dukkha**. There are two reasons why this is the case.

1. We rely on things to make us happy that let us down. Then we feel dissatisfied.

2. We do things that are selfish, thoughtless, or just plain stupid. In this way we create karma that will make us unhappy.

When we die, our karma is reborn again and again. Samsara is the cycle of karma through lifetimes of dukkha.

There are two ways to overcome dukkha.

1. People should overcome the tendency to rely on things to make them happy, and realise that happiness comes from inside themselves.

2. People need to do things that are motivated by love for others.

Buddhists say that their religion can help them do these two things. The state of peace and happiness that can come from this is called **nirvana**.

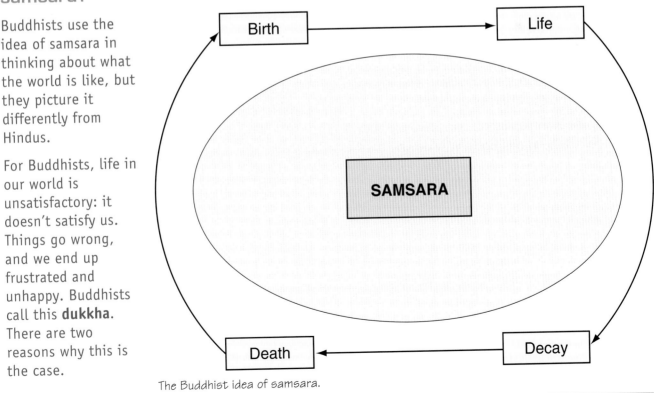

The Buddhist idea of samsara.

ACTIVITY ONE ·············

1. List all the things that went wrong yesterday.

2. List all the things that went right yesterday.

3. When did you last have a day when everything went right?

4. Do you agree with the Buddhist idea of samsara? Give examples from your own life to support your answer.

ACTIVITY TWO ················

Buddhism teaches that if you rely on things to make you happy, they will let you down and you will experience dukkha.

Think of five things, including animals and people, that make you happy. How could these same things make you unhappy?

ACTIVITY THREE ·············

On the following page are pictures of Brahma, Vishnu and Shiva, labelled 1, 2 and 3.

a) Match the pictures up with the descriptions given on this page.

b) Look at each picture carefully. What do they tell you about the characters of the gods?

c) Sometimes Brahma, Vishnu and Shiva are shown as three heads on one body. Why do you think this is so?

ⓘ What do Hindus believe about God?

Hindus think of God, not as a person, but as the force behind the entire universe. They call it **Brahman**. All beings come from Brahman, are part of Brahman, and return to Brahman. The three different aspects of Brahman are represented by three more personal gods.

Brahma

Brahma is called the Grandfather or the Creator, because he is responsible for the creation of all things. He does not create himself, but calls on another god, **Vishnu**, to do so. He is usually shown with four faces, to face in all directions; and with a book, a spoon, a flagon and a string of beads, which are all ritual objects.

Vishnu

Vishnu is the source and preserver of life. He is often shown lying in the coils of a seven-headed snake. He has four hands, and his skin is sky-blue, because, like the sky, he extends over the world. It is said that Vishnu appears on earth from time to time in various forms, called **avatars**, to bring about justice.

Shiva

Shiva is a terrifying destroyer god. He wears a tiger skin and snakes, and usually holds a weapon, an instrument of death. Yet Shiva's destructive energy paves the way for rebirth and new life.

Brahman enables each person to be born into the world, exist, and then pass away. A soul will be born again and again into different forms according to its karma. The idea is to work your way up through the various life forms, creating better and better karma, until your soul escapes from samsara and unites with God. This is called moksha (as we saw in lesson two of this unit).

ACTIVITY FOUR ·················

Draw a diagram to represent the Hindu idea of samsara.

First, think about what shape your diagram should be. It should include the atman, karma, the various life forms, and moksha.

NOW TRY THIS ··············

What are the differences between the Hindu and Buddhist ideas of samsara?

Use the words atman, moksha and nirvana in your answer.

KEY WORDS

Avatar   a Hindu god in a physical body (Hinduism)

Brahma   the creator god (Hinduism)

Brahman   God, the power behind the universe (Hinduism)

Dukkha   unhappiness and dissatisfaction (Buddhism)

Nirvana   the state of peace and happiness that results from overcoming desires (Buddhism)

Samsara   the cycle of birth, death and rebirth (Hinduism, Buddhism)

Shiva   the destroyer god (Hinduism)

Vishnu   the preserver god (Hinduism)

SUMMARY OF UNIT 5

Lesson 2

You have learned about Hindu and Sikh beliefs about the soul, and the Buddhist view that there is no soul.

Lesson 3

You have learned about the Christian view of free will, and the Muslim idea of predestination.

Lesson 1

You have learned about what Jews, Christians and Muslims believe human beings are, and their relationship with other living things.

What does religion say about being human?

Lesson 4

You have learned about what Hindus and Buddhists believe about karma, and how this influences their views about life after death.

Lesson 6

You have learned about Hindu beliefs about the relationship between God and the world, and about Hindu and Buddhist ideas of samsara.

Lesson 5

You have learned about Christian teachings about the existence of evil, and thought about what makes something evil.

UNIT 6: HOW DOES RELIGION AFFECT HUMAN BEHAVIOUR?

Lesson 1: What is worship?

◎ Read about the meaning of worship.

◎ Think about how people show respect.

◎ Discover ways in which religious people worship and compare these rituals with secular (non-religious) examples.

◎ Consider the idea of value and how you treat things that are valuable to you.

Lesson 2: What is prayer?

◎ Learn about the purpose of prayer for Christians.

◎ Find out how Muslims pray.

◎ Discover why prayer is important in Islam.

◎ Read about how people meditate and try a simple meditation exercise.

Lesson 3: What are ethics and morality?

◎ Work out what moral statements are about.

◎ Decide whether moral statements are absolute or relative.

◎ Find out how people make moral decisions.

◎ Read and interpret some people's views on morality, and form your own opinion.

Lesson 4: What do Christians, Jews and Muslims say about ethics and morality?

◎ Find out why religious people are concerned with morality.

◎ Read about the six moral commandments of Judaism and Christianity.

◎ Learn about Islamic moral teachings.

◎ Think about how to solve moral dilemmas, and compose one of your own.

Lesson 5: What do Hindus, Sikhs and Buddhists say about ethics and morality?

◎ Read about the Hindu idea of dharma.

◎ Think about responsibilities in the different stages of life.

◎ Find out about equality in Sikhism and other religions.

◎ Read about the Five Precepts of Buddhism.

◎ Discuss the Golden Rule and produce a pamphlet to illustrate it in action.

Lesson 6: How has religion affected the lives of individuals?

◎ Read about the lives of key religious people.

◎ Find out how religious belief has affected their lives.

◎ Discover how religious people's lives have affected the world.

How does religion affect human behaviour?

1. What is worship?

SKILLS

- **describing** examples of religious worship
- **linking** examples of religious rituals with secular ones
- **thinking about** things that are important to you and how you treat them
- **explaining** how and why people treat things they care about with respect

ACTIVITY ONE

Describe what you think is happening in pictures 1–8.

ⓘ What does worship mean?

When we say that something is valuable, we mean that it is important to us. It could be that it is worth a lot of money (*financial value*), or we could have an emotional tie to it (*sentimental value*). In either case, our attitude to it will be one of respect, and we will show that in the way we treat it.

Religious people show their respect for what is important to them in praise and worship. The word 'worship' means 'make worthy', in other words, to show the worth of something. The word 'praise' means the same sort of thing: 'to set a price on' something.

ACTIVITY TWO

1. Link pictures A–H (of **secular** forms of ritual), with pictures 1–8.

2. Describe what the link is in each case.

ACTIVITY THREE ••

Think of five things that are valuable to you. For each of them say:

a) why it is valuable, and

b) how your treatment of it shows its value.

We show our respect for valuable things in different ways.

ACTIVITY FOUR ••••••••••••••

Write a paragraph explaining how people show respect for things they value. In your paragraph, include the following:

• an explanation of the two different types of value (financial and sentimental)

• examples of each type

• an explanation of why people would want to treat things of value with care

• examples of how people treat things of value with care.

NOW TRY THIS ••••••••••••

People often show their respect for other people, or objects, by placing them higher up. With a partner:

a) list as many examples as you can think of where this is done;

b) try to think of different explanations for doing it.

2. What is prayer?

SKILLS

* **matching** biblical quotations with the purposes of Christian prayer
* **defining** Arabic words connected with Islamic prayer
* **explaining** why prayer is important for Muslims
* **experiencing** a meditation exercise
* **reflecting** on your feelings towards other people

ⓘ What is prayer?

Prayer is the way in which believers in God make contact with him. It may take the form of words spoken aloud, or silent thoughts and reflection. Silent thoughts and reflection are sometimes called **meditation**.

Different religions emphasise different functions of prayer.

Christianity

Christians highlight four main purposes of prayer.

1. Showing respect for God (**adoration**).

2. Admitting wrongdoings (**confession**).

3. Thanking God (**thanksgiving**).

4. Asking for God's help and guidance (**intercession**).

ACTIVITY ONE ·····················

Link each of the following quotations from the Christian Bible with one of the four purposes of Christian prayer, on the left.

a) *'If we confess our sins, he is faithful and just and will forgive us our sins and purify us from all unrighteousness.'*

(1 John 1:9)

b) *'Always giving thanks to God the Father for everything, in the name of our Lord Jesus Christ.'*

(Ephesians 5:20)

c) *'"Ask and it will be given to you; seek and you will find; knock and the door will be opened to you."'*

(Matthew 7:7)

d) *'May the peoples praise you, O God; may all the peoples praise you.'*

(Psalm 67:3)

▶ *What is this girl using to help her to pray?*

Islam

Muslims are encouraged to pray five times each day. This is called **salah**. A man called a **mu'adhin** calls people to prayer by reciting the **adhan** in Arabic:

Allahu Akbar ('Allah is Great', said four times).

Ashhadu an la ilaha illa Allah ('I bear witness that there is no god except the One God (Allah)', said twice).

Ashadu anna Muhammadan Rasool Allah ('I bear witness that Muhammad is the messenger of Allah', said twice).

Hayya 'ala-s-Salah ('Hurry to the prayer', said twice).

Hayya 'ala-l-Falah ('Hurry to success', said twice).

Muslims wash thoroughly before prayer by performing **wudu**. Salah itself is divided into **rakahs**, units of set prayers accompanied by a sequence of standing, bowing and kneeling forwards.

Each rakah is accompanied by a series of prayer positions.

ACTIVITY TWO

Write a definition of each of the following words:

adhan   mu'adhin   rakah   salah   wudu

ACTIVITY THREE

Read the following quotations from the Qur'an. Each one reveals a different purpose for prayer. Can you identify all five purposes?

1. 'Say [oh, Muhammad!]: "If you love Allah, follow me: Allah will forgive you your sins, for Allah is Oft-forgiving, Most Merciful."'

(Surah 3:31)

2. '"What led you into the Hell-fire?" They will say: "We were not of those who prayed."'

(Surah 74:42–43)

3. 'Successful indeed are the Believers, those who humble themselves in their prayers.'

(Surah 23:1–2)

4. 'And those who guard [strictly] their worship, such will be the honoured ones in the Gardens [of Bliss].'

(Surah 70:34–35)

5. '"Praise be to Allah, Lord of the worlds, the Compassionate, the Merciful, Master of the Day of Judgment. You only do we worship and to you only we cry for help. Guide us to the straight path, the path of those on whom you have bestowed your mercy."'

(Surah 1:1–7)

Buddhism

Buddhists, of course, don't believe in a creator-God, and so do not pray in the way that other religious people do. They are more likely to meditate. Meditation is a way of focusing the mind by filling it with thoughts of loving-kindness, compassion, happiness and peace. The idea is to share these feelings with all other beings. Buddhists who are well-practised in meditation use it to see the realities of life at a very deep level.

▲ Buddhists sometimes sit cross-legged in the 'lotus position' when they meditate.

▶ Sometimes they meditate while walking.

ACTIVITY FOUR

Try this simple meditation. It is not a religious activity, though some Buddhists do it. It is a method of relaxing the mind in preparation for Buddhist meditation.

1. Sit comfortably, so you are unlikely to fidget. Close your eyes, so you don't get distracted.

2. Think of yourself – not in detail, but just imagine you. Say to yourself, 'I wish me well. I wish myself to be free of unhappiness and suffering.' Say this over and over for about a minute.

3. Now reflect on how you feel.

4. Think of loved ones – family and friends. Say to yourself, 'I wish them well. I wish them all to be free of unhappiness and suffering.' Repeat it for about a minute.

5. Reflect on how you feel.

6. Think of acquaintances – people you know a bit, but not well. Say to yourself, 'I wish them well. I wish them all to be free of unhappiness and suffering.'

7. Reflect on how you feel.

8. Think of everyone in the whole world – whether you know them or not, whether you like them or not. Say to yourself, 'I wish them well. I wish them all to be free of unhappiness and suffering.'

9. Reflect on how you feel.

10. Slowly open your eyes, and reflect on how you feel.

NOW TRY THIS

a) Many people who aren't religious think that it's important for people to talk about the things they've done wrong, share their feelings with others and express their gratitude for happiness in their lives.

   (i) What's the difference between doing this and praying?

   (ii) Do you agree that people should talk openly about their feelings? Give reasons for your answer.

b) Many people who are not religious pray in times of crisis. Why do you think this is?

3. What are ethics and morality?

SKILLS

- **identifying** moral statements
- **reflecting** on what is right and wrong
- **thinking about** the ethics of killing
- **conducting** a survey about attitudes to right and wrong
- **deciding** whether you agree or disagree with certain views

KEY WORDS

Ethics   standards of right and wrong
Morality   right and wrong behaviour

ⓘ Ethics and morality

The words **ethics** and **morality** are often used to mean the same thing. They are about what is right and wrong, good and bad, and how human beings ought and ought not to behave.

ACTIVITY ONE ····················

Which of the following statements are concerned with morality?

Brussels sprouts are good for you.

You ought to brush your teeth every day.

You shouldn't talk to strangers.

It is wrong to steal.

Always tell the truth.

You must not run in the corridor.

Good Christians go to church on Sundays.

No smoking!

ACTIVITY TWO ·······························

1. Draw two columns, and head the first one 'Right' and the second one 'Wrong'.

2. In the first column, write down five *ethical* things that it is right for people to do; in the second, write five things that it is *wrong* to do.

3. Swap your lists with a partner.

4. Are there any statements that you could move from one column to another? Which ones? Why?

All people agree that it is wrong to break a promise; yet many may think it is sometimes the right thing to do. All people agree that it is good to tell the truth; but some may be able to see times when it is the wrong thing to do.

ACTIVITY THREE

Is it ever right to kill? How do you decide? Which of these actions do you think are right, and which are wrong? Try to give reasons for your answers. Discuss them in small groups.

- To kill an enemy soldier in war.
- To kill a person who is attacking you.
- To kill a person who asks you to.
- To kill a person in order to steal from them.
- To kill a mass murderer as a punishment.
- To kill a person whose body has stopped working.
- To kill a person who is in unbearable pain.
- To kill a person who has killed someone you love.

How did you make your decisions?

ACTIVITY FOUR

Conduct a survey in your class or year group. Ask people the question, 'How do you decide what is right and what is wrong?' They should choose their answer from the following options.

1. I do whatever feels right in the situation.
2. I use values that I have learned from my parents.
3. I use values that I have learned in school.
4. I use religious principles.
5. I do whatever produces the best results for me.
6. I do whatever makes most people happy.
7. I do whatever my family and friends expect of me.
8. I do whatever I would like done to me.

Try to present the results of your survey as percentages, or in a bar chart.

What conclusions can you draw from your survey?

NOW TRY THIS

Read through the following quotations about ethics and morality. Choose three of them and explain, in your own words, what they mean. Then say whether you agree or disagree with them, and why.

'When I do good, I feel good; when I do bad, I feel bad. That's my religion.'

(President Abraham Lincoln)

'The only thing necessary for the triumph of Evil is for good men to do nothing.'

(Edmund Burke)

'Of moral purpose I see no trace in Nature. That is an article of exclusively human manufacture – and very much to our credit.'

(Thomas Henry Huxley)

'A man does what he must – in spite of personal consequences, in spite of obstacles and dangers and pressures – and that is the basis of all morality.'

(John Fitzgerald Kennedy)

'There is nothing either good or bad, but thinking makes it so.'

William Shakespeare

4. What do Christians, Jews and Muslims say about ethics and morality?

SKILLS

- **comparing** Christian and Islamic writings about ethics
- **matching** quotations from the Qur'an with commandments from the Bible
- **analysing** moral dilemmas
- **composing** your own moral dilemma

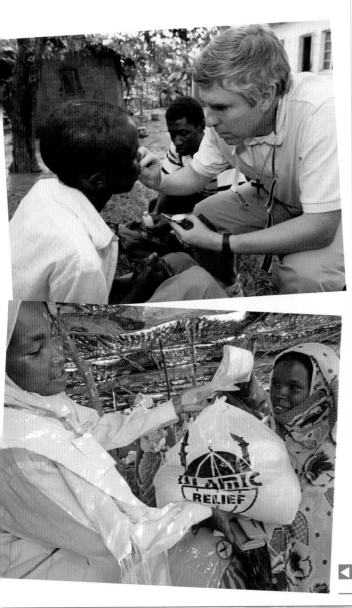

ACTIVITY ONE ··················

Read these two passages carefully. The first is from the Christian Bible, and the second from the Qur'an.

'Then the King will say …, "Come, you who are blessed by my Father; take your inheritance, the kingdom prepared for you since the creation of the world. For I was hungry and you gave me something to eat, I was thirsty and you gave me something to drink, I was a stranger and you invited me in, I needed clothes and you clothed me, I was sick and you looked after me, I was in prison and you came to visit me."

Then the righteous will answer him, "Lord, when did we do these things?"

The King will reply, "I tell you the truth, whatever you did for one of the least of these brothers of mine, you did for me."'

(Adapted from Matthew 25:34–40)

'It is not righteousness that you turn your faces towards the East and the West, but righteousness is this: that one should believe in Allah, and the last day, and the angels, and the Book, and the prophets; and give away wealth out of love for Him to your relations and orphans and the needy and the traveller and beggars and for the freeing of captives, and keep up prayer and give to charity … these are the true believers, the God-fearing.'

(Qur'an 2:177)

What do they have in common?

◀ *Why do religious people get involved in charity work?*

Christians and Jews believe that God gave them specific rules on how to behave.
They are the last six of the Ten Commandments.

'Honour your father and your mother, so that you may live long in the land the LORD your God is giving you.

You shall not murder.

You shall not commit adultery.

You shall not steal.

You shall not give false testimony [evidence] against your neighbour.

You shall not covet [crave] your neighbour's house. You shall not covet your neighbour's wife, or his … servant, his ox or donkey, or anything that belongs to your neighbour.'

(Exodus 20:12–17)

Similar commandments appear in the Qur'an.

'And do not kill anybody that Allah has prohibited except when you have a right to kill.'

(Surah 6:151)

'As to the thief (man or woman) let their hands be cut off, a retaliation for what they did, a punishment from Allah.'

(Surah 5:38)

'And do not even go near adultery. It is a vile sin and evil behaviour.'

(Surah 17:32)

'Do good to your parents. If they reach old age before your eyes, any one of them or both, then do not say a word of criticism to them and do not scold them; rather speak kindly to them.'

(Surah 17:23–24)

'And do not long for those things with which Allah has favoured some of you over others.'

(Surah 4:32)

'Do not withhold any testimony by concealing what you had witnessed. Anyone who withholds a testimony is sinful at heart.'

(Surah 2:283)

ACTIVITY TWO ....

Match up the quotations from the Qur'an with the commandments from the Jewish and Christian Bibles.

Following ethical codes, like commandments, is fine when things are simple; but they rarely are. A **moral dilemma** is a situation that requires a choice between two options, neither of which will have a desirable outcome. On the next page are some examples.

1

Abdul was bouncing a ball against a wall at school. One throw was too hard, and in the wrong direction. Abdul smashed a window. No one saw him do it.

Now his friend, Ali, is being blamed for it. He may get excluded.

2

George is 84 years old. He is suffering from cancer. It started in his stomach, and spread to his liver and colon. The doctors say he has only a couple of months to live.

Meanwhile, George is in constant pain. He can't get out of bed, and can't bear the thought that his wife, Ellen, should watch him suffer. He wants to die and has asked Ellen to help him do it.

3

Leah is 11 years old. When she was born, she was very ill, and her life was in danger for the first five years. She could not walk until she was eight. Now she is well, and her parents are very proud of her. In their opinion, she can do no wrong.

One day, her sister, Amy, sees Leah stealing some sweets from a shop, though Leah doesn't know Amy has seen. The girls' parents would be heartbroken if they found out.

ACTIVITY FOUR ················

Go through the three scenarios again. This time, write down:

a) Which of the moral commandments (those listed on the previous page) is relevant.

b) How the commandments might help in making a decision.

ACTIVITY THREE ··············

Discuss each of the three scenarios with a partner. For each one, write down:

a) Who has the moral dilemma?

b) What is the dilemma?

c) What the person should do, in your opinion.

d) Reasons why the person should do this.

NOW TRY THIS ··············

Think of your own moral dilemma. It might be a real one that you have had to face. Then explain how a belief in the moral commandments might help you solve it.

5. What do Hindus, Sikhs and Buddhists say about ethics and morality?

SKILLS

- **identifying** your own duties and responsibilities
- **discussing** the Hindu dharma
- **investigating** the idea of equality in some of the world's religions
- **inferring** how Buddhist ethical beliefs might affect job choices

ACTIVITY ONE

1. What duties and responsibilities do you have at your age?

2. What are the differences between being a young person and an adult?

Hinduism

Hindus believe that actions are wrong when they harm other beings. Because of the law of karma, they believe that wrong actions come back to affect them. The way that Hindus should behave depends on their **dharma**. Dharma means 'duty'. Each person has his or her own dharma according to the stage of life (**ashrama**) they are at. There are four ashramas.

ⓘ The four ashramas

1. Student. Up to the age of about 20, a young person should develop his or her character by learning from those who are older and wiser.

2. Householder. From the age of 20 to about 50, a person should build up a career, get married, have children, and provide for the family.

3. Hermit. After a person's children have grown up, he or she need no longer provide for them, but should spend time studying and worshipping.

4. Holy man (**sadhu**). A sadhu is a person who does not follow the path of a householder, but seeks to develop spiritually through religious practices.

What duties do people have at different stages of life?

ACTIVITY TWO

Discuss with a partner some of the benefits of each ashrama, and some of the drawbacks.

Sikhism

Sikhs, like Hindus, believe in karma. They believe that the actions you take in your daily life will affect your life in the future. But they don't agree that a person's life should be affected by the class they are born into, the colour of their skin, their nationality, their sex, the way they speak, or even their religion. They believe that everyone is equal in every respect.

The Gurus were particularly concerned that women were thought to be inferior to men in society and in religious organisations. Guru Nanak wrote:

'We are born of woman, we are conceived in the womb of woman, we are engaged and married to woman. We make friendship with woman and the lineage continues because of woman. When one woman dies, we take another one. We are bound to the world through woman. Why should we talk ill of her, who gives birth to kings? The woman is born from woman, there is none without her.'

(Guru Nanak, *Var Asa*)

ACTIVITY THREE ....

Conduct a survey of the role of women in the world's religions from pictures in RE textbooks. Pick 20 photographs at random of people involved in religious activities from two or three books.

a) How many pictures have men in positions of leadership, and how many have women?

b) What sorts of things are men doing in the pictures?

c) What sorts of things are women doing?

d) What can you conclude from this?

▶ *One way that Sikhs show their belief in equality is by eating together.*

Buddhism

Buddhists also believe that everyone is equal, because everyone is connected. In a sense, they say, we don't have individual lives. There is one life that we all share. Therefore, whatever we do affects us as much as it affects others (karma).

ⓘ Buddhist guidelines

Buddhists have guidelines to help them decide the wisest thing to do. They are known as the **Five Precepts**.

1. To avoid killing.

2. To avoid stealing.

3. To avoid using sex harmfully.

4. To avoid telling untruths.

5. To avoid drugs and alcohol that cloud the mind.

ACTIVITY FOUR

If a person tried to follow the Five Precepts, how would it affect his or her working life? List ten jobs they would be unlikely to have and then jobs they would want to have. Here are two ideas to get you started.

NOW TRY THIS

All religions agree that you treat other people in the way that you would want to be treated. Many non-religious people agree. It is called the **Golden Rule**.

Design a leaflet or poster to promote the Golden Rule in your school. Try to find out how it is worded in a variety of religions. Use the different wordings and draw some illustrations as examples of the Golden Rule in action.

KEY WORDS

Ashrama   one of four stages of life (Hinduism)
Dharma   duty (Hinduism)
Five Precepts   guidelines for moral behaviour (Buddhism)
Golden Rule   the rule that advises people to treat others in the same way that they would want to be treated themselves
Sadhu   a holy man (Hinduism)

6. How has religion affected the lives of individuals?

SKILLS

- **investigating** the life of an influential religious person
- **planning** your assignment
- **analysing** the link between religious belief and behaviour
- **interpreting** quotes from and about a religious person
- **expressing** your own views about a person's life and work

ACTIVITY

Task

You have been asked to design a website celebrating the life of a religious person whose life has made a difference in the world. You can choose whomever you like – some suggestions are given on the following pages – but the person must be someone whose religion has made a difference in their life, and whose life has made a difference in the world.

Guidelines

Your website should consist of at least three pages, and include the following.

1. A biography (life-story) of the person. Concentrate particularly on events that have influenced the history of the world.

2. Some quotations from and about the person. These should explain how the person's beliefs have influenced their lives.

3. Personal reflection on the person's life. Think about what has impressed you about the person, both in their character and in what they have achieved. Think, too, about ways in which they could have acted differently.

Try to include photographs of the person at various stages in their career.

You could present your assignment as an MS Word document, or as a handwritten draft, or even on your school website.

If you don't want to design a website, you could produce a leaflet or magazine article.

◀ *Some religious people have had a great influence on the world. These* Time *magazine covers show (from top to bottom) Martin Luther King, Mahatma Gandhi and the Dalai Lama.*

Some religious figures to investigate

Mahatma Gandhi (Hindu) – Indian spiritual and political leader.

Oscar Romero (Christian) – Salvadoran archbishop and martyr.

Dalai Lama (Buddhist) – Head of state and spiritual leader of the Tibetan people.

Martin Luther King (Christian) – African-American civil rights leader.

Malcolm X (Muslim) – African-American civil rights leader.

Bhimrao Ramji Ambedkar (Buddhist) – Indian social reformer, politician.

Prabhupada A.C. Bhaktivedanta (Hindu) – Indian founder of ISKCON.

▲ *Yusuf Islam (Muslim) –
British former pop singer.*

▲ *Theodore Hertzl (Jewish) –
Founder of Zionist movement.*

▲ *Simon Wiesenthal (Jewish) –
Holocaust survivor and Nazi hunter.*

▲ *Sant Jarnail Singh
Bhindranwale
(Sikh) – Indian
politician and
martyr.*

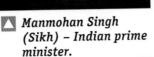

▲ *Manmohan Singh
(Sikh) – Indian prime
minister.*

▲ *Bob Marley (Rastafarian) –
Reggae musician.*

▶ *Elizabeth Fry
(Christian) –
Campaigner for prison
reform.*

NOW TRY THIS ....

Find out about another person, working in the
same field as your original subject, but from a
different religious background. Compare their
beliefs and actions.

SUMMARY OF UNIT 6

Lesson 2

You have learned about why Christians and Muslims pray, and how some people meditate.

Lesson 3

You have learned about what distinguishes a moral statement, and how people make moral decisions.

Lesson 1

You have learned about how people show respect for things that they value, and the ways in which religious people worship.

How does religion affect human behaviour?

Lesson 4

You have learned about how Jews, Christians and Muslims may make moral decisions, and what moral dilemmas are.

Lesson 6

You have learned about the life of a famous religious person, and about how that person's actions were influenced by their religious beliefs.

Lesson 5

You have learned about duty in Hinduism, and how Buddhists are guided in their moral thinking.

Glossary

Abhidamma Buddhist scripture explaining the Buddha's teachings in detail

Absolute fixed or set

Adhan the Islamic call to prayer

Adi Granth the first Sikh holy book, compiled by the fifth guru

Adoration expression of love and respect in worship

Allegory a story that teaches people about life

Amrit Sanskar the Sikh ceremony of baptism and initiation

Analogy comparing a complicated idea with something more simple and familiar, to help explain it

Anatta the idea that a fixed, permanent identity is an illusion (Buddhism)

Apocrypha 14 Jewish books not included in the Tenakh, but included in some versions of the Christian Bible

Argument the statement of a belief backed up by reasons

Ark a cupboard in a synagogue where sacred scrolls are kept

Artefact a human-made object

Ashrama one of four stages of life (Hinduism)

Atheist a person who does not believe in a God

Atman the soul (Hinduism)

Authority 1. the power one person may have over another; 2. an expert

Avatar a Hindu god in a physical body (Hinduism)

Baisakhi Sikh festival to mark the founding of the Khalsa

Baptism a ceremony to mark a new beginning

Bible the Christian holy book

Bhikkhu a Buddhist monk

Brahma the creator god (Hinduism)

Brahman God, the power behind the universe (Hinduism)

Buddha a person who is enlightened and understands life at a very deep level

Caliph one of the successors to Muhammad (Islam)

Chanani canopy under which the Guru Granth Sahib rests when being read

Chauri whisk or fan waved over the Guru Granth Sahib to protect it

Church 1. a Christian place of worship; 2. the community of Christians worldwide

Circumcision the removal of the foreskin of the penis to welcome a boy to Judaism or Islam

Confession admitting wrong doings

Confirmation a ceremony in which a person becomes a full member of a religious organisation, especially the Christian Church

Conservative a person who believes that the Bible is the word of God, but has been interpreted by human beings

Denomination a branch of the Christian Church

Dhammapada Buddhist scripture containing sayings of the Buddha

Dharma duty (Hinduism)

Dimension one of the seven characteristics of a world-view

Divali Hindu festival of lights

Dukkha unhappiness and dissatisfaction (Buddhism)

Easter Christian festival that commemorates the Resurrection of Jesus

Empirical able to be experienced through the senses

Empowered given power and authority

Enlightenment the state of being enlightened

Ethics standards of right and wrong

Evidence a collection of reasons

Five Ks symbolic objects worn by Sikhs

Five Precepts   guidelines for moral behaviour (Buddhism)

Genetic   to do with the characteristics that are passed from parents to children during reproduction

Golden Rule   the rule that advises people to treat others in the same way as they would want to be treated themselves

Gospels   four accounts of the life and teachings of Jesus in the Christian Bible

Granthi   the person who looks after the Guru Granth Sahib (Sikhism)

Guru   a spiritual teacher

Guru Granth Sahib   the Sikh holy book

Hebrew   the language of the Jewish Bible

Hypothesis   a scientific theory or prediction

Id-ul-Fitr   Islamic festival to mark the end of Ramadan

Imam   the person who leads Islamic worship

Intercession   prayer asking for God's help, especially for other people

Irrational   having no reasons

Jataka   stories about the Buddha's previous lives

Karma   (action) the idea that your actions affect what will happen to you in the future

Ketuvim   'writings': the third section of the Jewish Bible

Khalsa   the community of Sikhs

Laws of Manu   collection of twelve Hindu books containing instructions in law and ethics

Liberal   a person who believes that the Bible was inspired by God, but is not to be taken as scientific fact

Literalist   a person who believes that the Bible is literally and scientifically true

Mantle   a covering for a Sefer Torah

Meditation   deep concentration

Mitzvah (mitzvot *pl.*)   commandments (Judaism)

Moksha   freedom from the cycle of birth and death (Hinduism)

Moral   to do with what is good, bad, right or wrong in human behaviour

Moral dilemma   a situation that requires a choice between two options, neither of which will have a desirable outcome

Morality   right and wrong behaviour

Mu'adhin   a person who calls people to prayer in Islam

Nevi'im   'prophets': the second section of the Jewish Bible

Nirvana   the state of peace and happiness that results from overcoming desires (Buddhism)

Orthodox   a strictly traditional form of Judaism

Overawed   filled with fear and wonder

Parable   a story told to illustrate another meaning or moral point

Pastoral   part of the work of religious leaders that involves looking after the people in their care

Pesach   Jewish festival to commemorate the freedom of the ancient Jewish people from slavery

Prayer   the way in which believers in God make contact with him

Priest   a religious leader with spiritual powers

Progressive   a liberal form of Judaism which believes in adapting religious practices to suit the times

Prophet   a person who believes he or she has a message from God

Qur'an   the holy book of Islam

Rabbi   a Jewish teacher

Rakah   a unit of prayer (Islam)

Ramadan   Islamic month of fasting

Ramayana   the story of Rama and Sita

Reason   a statement used to back up an opinion, belief or statement of knowledge

Reincarnation   the belief that the soul is reborn in another body

Relative changeable when compared to different things

Resurrection a rising of the dead (usually refers to Jesus Christ)

Sadhu a holy man (Hinduism)

Salah set prayers conducted five times a day (Islam)

Samsara the cycle of birth, death and rebirth (Hinduism, Buddhism)

Sanctity holiness, preciousness

Sangha the community of Buddhists worldwide, especially the community of Buddhist monks

Scribe a person who writes Jewish scrolls by hand

Sect a subdivision of a religious group

Secular non-religious

Seder a special meal held during the Jewish festival of Pesach

Sefer Torah a Torah scroll

Shi'ah Muslims who believe that Muhammad's son-in-law, Ali, was his true successor

Shiva the destroyer god (Hinduism)

Shruti *'what is heard'*; Hindu scriptures believed to have come from God

Smriti *'what is remembered'*; Hindu scriptures written to explain the Shruti

Spiritual to do with aspects of human life that cannot be experienced physically, like emotions and feelings

Subjective individual

Sunni Muslims who believe that Abu Bakr was Muhammad's true successor

Supervise to be in charge of something – organising and managing it

Sutta Buddhist scripture containing the Buddha's teaching

Swami a spiritual teacher or master (Hinduism)

Takht padded throne on which the Guru Granth Sahib rests when being read

Tenakh the Jewish holy book, sometimes called the Bible

Thanksgiving prayer thanking God for his goodness

Tipitaka the collection of Buddhist holy scriptures

Torah 'law' or 'teaching': the first, and most important section of the Jewish Bible

Ultimate questions important questions concerning what we believe about life

Ummah the Islamic community worldwide

Vedas the oldest of the Hindu holy books

Vinaya Buddhist scripture containing rules for monks and nuns

Vishnu the preserver god (Hinduism)

Wesak Buddhist festival to remember the birth, death and enlightenment of the Buddha

World-view the way a person or group of people sees and reacts to the world around them

Wudu ritual washing before salah

Yad a pointer used in reading Jewish scrolls

Index